Copyright©2020 by Laura Livingston Lewis

Scriptures quoted in this book were taken from the Bible, King James Version.

All rights reserved. No part of this publication may be reproduced, stored in a retrieval system via photocopying or recording, or transmitted in any form, except for review or promotional purposes, without the written permission by the Author or Publisher.

Published in the United States of America

First Edition

10987654321

ISBN 978-1 945450-13-6

Baird Farms Publishing Company LLC

Mount Juliet, TN 37122

wdjaq@aol.com

Dedication

This book is dedicated to my family. I can never thank God enough for giving me Parents who made sure their children were introduced to Jesus! My Daughters Lori, Laurette and LaChele, I love you all to Mercury, Venus, Jupiter and Mars and back again a thousand times! No end to my love. My precious Son, Jody, your presence in my heart has provided much comfort since you've been in Heaven! Precious Sisters Lana, Laurinda, Lamona, Londa and sweet Launette (in Heaven), then Brothers Larry, Lyman, Linton and LaVaughn, I'm so very glad we've had each other and have done Life together! Grandsons, Granddaughters, Nieces and Nephews plus all of the Greats? I care enough to remind you that your sweet PawPawd wore holes in the knees of his pants praying for his present family – plus any that he knew would come after he left for Heaven – that all of us would go there, too. Last but really most important, I dedicate this book to my Other Half, Ray Lewis, who now lives in Heaven. He believed in me as a person, wife, friend, author and songwriter. He always publicly referred to me as his pride........and his Barbie ☺. Because of his importance in my life as well as the impact he made on so many others, I have mentioned him several times in my book. I'm evermore grateful for the time God gave us together!

Laura

Table of Contents

Week 1	Magnify Monday	2
	Trust Tuesday	3
	Warm Wednesday	4
	Try Thursday	5
	First Friday	6
	Secret Saturday	7
	Shepherd Sunday	8
Week 2	Mad Monday	10
	Together Tuesday	11
	Weave Wednesday	12
	Trophy Thursday	13
	Fleeting Friday	14
	Surmount Saturday	15
	Sympathize Sunday	16
Week 3	Meritable Monday	18
	Tardy Tuesday	19
	Wallow Wednesday	20
	Trove Thursday	21
	Fascinating Friday	22
	Spectacular Saturday	23
	Strengthen Sunday	24
Week 4	More Monday	26
	Tarry Tuesday	27
	Watermelon Wednesday	28
	Tremendous Thursday	29
	Finish Friday	30
	Shipshape Saturday	31
	Shoulder Sunday	32
Week 5	Manna Monday	34
	There Tuesday	35
	Write Wednesday	36
	Tidy Thursday	37
	Fireball Friday	38
	Shirker Saturday	39
	Stupendous Sunday	40
Week 6	Milestone Monday	42
	Treasure Tuesday	43
	Withstand Wednesday	44

	Tolerant Thursday	45
	Forgotten Friday	46
	Simple Saturday	47
	Serve Sunday	48
Week 7	Marvelous Monday	50
	Topnotch Tuesday	51
	Whoopee Wednesday	52
	Team Thursday	53
	Fair Friday	54
	Striking Saturday	55
	Symphony Sunday	56
Week 8	Miracle Monday	58
	Tiller Tuesday	59
	Warrior Wednesday	60
	Transmission Thursday	61
	Funny Friday	62
	Silly Saturday	63
	Shower Sunday	64
Week 9	Moving Monday	66
	Thrive Tuesday	67
	Wait Wednesday	68
	Tend Thursday	69
	Family Friday	70
	Storm Saturday	71
	Shake Sunday	72
Week 10	Major Monday	74
	Talk Tuesday	75
	Wise Wednesday	76
	Tall Thursday	77
	Forward Friday	78
	Suitable Saturday	79
	Selective Sunday	80
Week 11	Millionaire Monday	82
	Tickled Tuesday	83
	Wean Wednesday	84
	Tone Thursday	85
	Friendly Friday	86
	Stage Saturday	87
	Star Sunday	88
Week 12	Monotony Monday	90
	Technique Tuesday	91
	Whiz Wednesday	92

	Tribute Thursday	93
	Flaw Friday	94
	Saddle Saturday	95
	Saved Sunday	96
Week 13	Masterpiece Monday	98
	Tempo Tuesday	99
	Wisdom Wednesday	100
	Temper Thursday	101
	Fruitful/Fruitless Friday	102
	Serviceable Saturday	103
	Soothe Sunday	104
Week 14	Musical Monday	106
	Turn Tuesday	107
	Where Wednesday	108
	Thorough Thursday	109
	Fresh Friday	110
	Soaring Saturday	111
	Solitude Sunday	112
Week 15	Moral Monday	114
	Toughest Tuesday	115
	Whosoever Wednesday	116
	Trader Thursday	117
	Fellowship Friday	118
	Superexcellent Saturday	119
	Sabotage Sunday	120
Week 16	Me Monday	122
	Terrific Tuesday	123
	Weather Wednesday	124
	Total Thursday	125
	Fabulous Friday	126
	Surprising Saturday	127
	Send Sunday	128
Week 17	Motivation Monday	130
	Tenacity Tuesday	131
	Witness Wednesday	132
	Twiddle Thursday	133
	Folks Friday	134
	Sandbox Saturday	135
	Stretch Sunday	136
Week 18	Majority Monday	138
	Trash Tuesday	139
	Warmhearted Wednesday	140

	Twinge Thursday	141
	Fantastic Friday	142
	Sandwich Saturday	143
	Supreme Sunday	144
Week 19	Mirth Monday	146
	Tact Tuesday	147
	Wonderful Wednesday	148
	Tunnel Thursday	149
	Finally Friday	150
	Stirring Saturday	151
	Surrender Sunday	152
Week 20	Magnetic Monday	154
	Tour Tuesday	155
	Worthy Wednesday	156
	Trivia Thursday	157
	Flattering Friday	158
	Storage Saturday	159
	See Sunday	160
Week 21	Measure Monday	162
	Trample Tuesday	163
	Wholesome Wednesday	164
	Trim Thursday	165
	Forethought Friday	166
	Sack Saturday	167
	Salutary Sunday	168
Week 22	Magnanimous Monday	170
	Toil Tuesday	171
	Whisper Wednesday	172
	Treaty Thursday	173
	Flourish Friday	174
	Survey Saturday	175
	Spurring Sunday	176
Week 23	Magnitude Monday	178
	Twinkle Tuesday	179
	When Wednesday	180
	Tricky Thursday	181
	Forceful Friday	182
	Sensational Saturday	183
	Shouting Sunday	184
Week 24	Maximum Monday	186
	Tool Tuesday	187
	While Wednesday	188

	Treasurer Thursday	189
	Forthright Friday	190
	Synthetic Saturday	191
	Serene Sunday	192
Week 25	Modest Monday	194
	Take Tuesday	195
	Welcome Wednesday	196
	Trounce Thursday	197
	Fluffy Friday	198
	Swim Saturday	199
	Soul Sunday	200
Week 26	Merry Monday	202
	Toss Tuesday	203
	Windfall Wednesday	204
	Trestle Thursday	205
	Forbearance Friday	206
	Skipper Saturday	207
	Swap Sunday	208
Week 27	Majesty Monday	210
	Truth Tuesday	211
	Wrap Wednesday	212
	Trench Thursday	213
	Freedom Friday	214
	Singing Saturday	215
	Surpass Sunday	216
Week 28	Mission Monday	218
	Teacher Tuesday	219
	Warehouse Wednesday	220
	Thorn Thursday	221
	Fulfill Friday	222
	Safe Saturday	223
	Synonymous Sunday	224
Week 29	Mirror Monday	226
	Trait Tuesday	227
	Willing Wednesday	228
	Treadmill Thursday	229
	Famous Friday	230
	Sapphire Saturday	231
	Splendid Sunday	232
Week 30	Mighty Monday	234
	Taboo Tuesday	235
	Whetting Wednesday	236

	Tactics Thursday	237
	Functional Friday	238
	Stunning Saturday	239
	Separate Sunday	240
Week 31	Magniloquence Monday	242
	Thrilling Tuesday	243
	Wall Wednesday	244
	Talent Thursday	245
	Forgiveness Friday	246
	Sparkle Saturday	247
	Sword Sunday	248
Week 32	Marshal Monday	250
	Task Tuesday	251
	What Wednesday	252
	Truce Thursday	253
	Flat Friday	254
	Superb Saturday	255
	Swerve Sunday	256
Week 33	Messenger Monday	258
	Transmit Tuesday	259
	Why Wednesday	260
	Trend Thursday	261
	Firm Friday	262
	Signboard Saturday	263
	Somehow Sunday	264
Week 34	Meantime Monday	266
	Transition Tuesday	267
	Waterloo Wednesday	268
	Tug Thursday	269
	Forge Friday	270
	Scheme Saturday	271
	Sweetheart Sunday	272
Week 35	Meditative Monday	274
	Train Tuesday	275
	Wrinkle Wednesday	276
	Tag Thursday	277
	Flamboyant Friday	278
	Self-Sufficient Saturday	279
	Sovereign Sunday	280
Week 36	Mistakes Monday	282
	Touch Tuesday	283
	Wealthy Wednesday	284

	Today Thursday	285
	Feed Friday	286
	Subject Saturday	287
	Swallow Sunday	288
Week 37	Memorable Monday	290
	Transform Tuesday	291
	Winning Wednesday	292
	Tumble Thursday	293
	Fortunate Friday	294
	Seed Saturday	295
	Supple Sunday	296
Week 38	Meaningful Monday	298
	Temperament Tuesday	299
	Watch Wednesday	300
	Tempest Thursday	301
	Fitting Friday	302
	Shopping Saturday	303
	Subtract Sunday	304
Week 39	Meantime Monday	306
	Tranquil Tuesday	307
	Wakening Wednesday	308
	Treatment Thursday	309
	Forever Friday	310
	Sanction Saturday	311
	Ship Sunday	312
Week 40	Magnificent Monday	314
	Tortoise Tuesday	315
	Weigh Wednesday	316
	Trial Thursday	317
	Focus Friday	318
	Sashay Saturday	319
	Sunny Sunday	320
Week 41	Mannerly Monday	322
	Tonic Tuesday	323
	Wash Wednesday	324
	Tiptop Thursday	325
	Fence Friday	326
	Sublime Saturday	327
	Sift Sunday	328
Week 42	Mystery Monday	330
	Trawl Tuesday	331
	Walk Wednesday	332

	Triumphant Thursday	333
	Fitness Friday	334
	Seesaw Saturday	335
	Share Sunday	336
Week 43	Melodious Monday	338
	Transcend Tuesday	339
	World Wednesday	340
	Triple Thursday	341
	Flow Friday	342
	Still Saturday	343
	Smart Sunday	344
Week 44	Matchless Monday	346
	Tiptoe Tuesday	347
	Wonder Wednesday	348
	Thoughtful Thursday	349
	Faith Friday	350
	Sufficient Saturday	351
	Step Sunday	352
Week 45	Model Monday	354
	Tow Tuesday	355
	Well Wednesday	356
	Torch Thursday	357
	Fortitude Friday	358
	Situation Saturday	359
	Substitute Sunday	360
Week 46	Mold Monday	362
	This Tuesday	363
	Wary Wednesday	364
	Trouble Thursday	365
	Farewell Friday	366
	Style Saturday	367
	Study Sunday	368
Week 47	Mellow Monday	370
	Testament Tuesday	371
	Wet Wednesday	372
	Tweak Thursday	373
	Figure Friday	374
	Savory Saturday	375
	Same Sunday	376
Week 48	My Monday	378
	Trade Tuesday	379
	Warranty Wednesday	380

	Think Thursday	381
	Favor Friday	382
	Sweep Saturday	383
	State Sunday	384
Week 49	Momentum Monday	386
	Timely Tuesday	387
	Work Wednesday	388
	Tune Thursday	389
	Field Friday	390
	Schedule Saturday	391
	Sacred Sunday	392
Week 50	Monitor Monday	394
	Thumbs Tuesday	395
	Witty Wednesday	396
	Temple Thursday	397
	Favorite Friday	398
	Sustenance Saturday	399
	Sturdy Sunday	400
Week 51	Mountain Monday	402
	Threshold Tuesday	403
	Worship Wednesday	404
	Tackle Thursday	405
	Foundation Friday	406
	Surety Saturday	407
	Synergy Sunday	408
Week 52	Mindful Monday	410
	Twister Tuesday	411
	Wear Wednesday	412
	Tint Thursday	413
	Follow Friday	414
	Strong Saturday	415
	Seek Sunday	416
Holidays	New Year's Day	418
	Valentine's Day	419
	Easter	420
	Mother's Day	421
	Memorial Day	422
	Father's Day	423
	Independence Day	424
	Labor Day	425
	Halloween	426
	Thanksgiving Day	427

Christmas Day	428
New Year's Eve	429
Acknowledgements	430
About the Author	431

How This Book Came About

Throughout life, many people have honored me by telling me that I am an Encourager. I *do* say that I'm a Registered Optimist. In 2011 I began to see that different folks on Facebook needed encouragement, so I started sharing a paragraph of "Alliteration" titles like "Marvelous Monday," "Terrific Tuesday," "Wonderful Wednesday," that sort of thing. Folks responded really well, so I made it part of my morning Devotion Time to write them every morning for a month or two. Then one day I found myself in the southeastern mountains of Oklahoma where there was no cell service, so I couldn't continue doing what I'd started. When I arrived home a few days later, I was out of the routine of sharing with FB Friends every morning, so I stopped writing them. I was surprised when a lot of folks contacted me to ask when I was going to begin again, telling me that they missed them. It was those very words from different folks that inspired me to put all my "Blurbs" in a book. It has taken me a while to bring it to fruition, but it's always better late than never. My heartfelt thanks to all the Friends on Facebook who gave me inspiration to achieve a new goal. I'm grateful to you all.

Introduction

We all have days that are reminiscent of Roller Coaster rides, up and down and all around, both fun and a little scary. Sometimes Life can be like those rides, but they do their part in molding us into the person we are today.

This book presents help in making Life choices. Our Creator gave us free will and that's what it's for, to make choices, both big and small. My hope is that the Blurbs on any given page will help you make choices when The Unexpected "drops in" on you throughout your journey on earth. My background/degree for writing this book came from the University of Life; God has been my Professor. I still attend that college today, and He is still my Professor. It has been His Holy Spirit giving me many things to say to you, and I have spoken them from my heart, as if you were sitting right here beside me. Some of the encouraging words are small parts of songs I have written.

My aspirations for a positive outlook started when I was in Junior High and read the classic, "Pollyanna." After finishing the book, I was determined to "be" one; a Pollyanna.

Pollyanna's mother died when she was very young, so her father, a minister, raised her alone until he, too, passed away when she was eleven years old. His legacy to her was the "Glad Game." They played it together every day. The rule of the game was simply to *find at least one thing* they could be glad about in *any* situation, no matter how daunting.

Pollyanna continued the game after she was placed with her aunt, who was never happy, always complaining. Pollyanna was glad she had the Glad Game to carry her through those teenage years, plus it accompanied her through the remainder of her Life. I am thankful I read that book, because God, humor (Thank you, Heavenly Father, for the capacity to laugh ☺!) and Pollyanna's Glad Game, helped me to cope with many hurdles through the years. I found there was *always* a way to turn a Negative to a Positive. This was my choice, you see. Your choice, too…

Week 1

Today is Magnify Monday!

Today is MAGNIFY MONDAY! To Magnify is "to praise highly." The first One we'd better praise is the God of all creation! So much to praise Him for, after all. Waking up, air to breathe, Life awaits! After that, we can make a habit of praising our children for the right things they do, as well as spouses, postman, supermarket clerk, etc. Don't do it expecting to get praise in return; just Magnify! Have a great Monday!

Today is Trust Tuesday!

Today is TRUST TUESDAY! Today we have a lot of modern conveniences for almost anything we do. We Trust them to make the world go 'round. In pioneer days, folks had to trust their abilities, each other, but best of all, God. Great thing is – God's still here today making everything work, even when buttons won't! Just Trust…!

Today is Warm Wednesday!

Today is WARM WEDNESDAY! When it's cold outside, the biggest part of the population on earth is inside…and Warm. Those who must work outside wear special clothing to help keep them…warm. What about inside our heart…is it warm there? Or, is there a cold area when you think of a particular person or situation? Problems are made to be solved, and guess what…I know the Problem Solver! He can make any cold area in your life turn warm! Cold doesn't feel good when you need to be warm. Your choice: Cold? Or WARM?

Today is Try Thursday!

Today is TRY THURSDAY! Try today to do something new/positive that you've never done before. Try harder to get past a hurt. Try harder to forgive an enemy. Try harder to make your marriage work. Try harder to read more Bible. Try harder to put a smile on your face in "trying" times. Got a mountain too hard to climb? Try harder!!! Try, Try, Try. What an inspiring word in itself, don't you think?

Today is First Friday!

Today is FIRST FRIDAY! First Friday of the month obviously; so, let's COPY it by doing some firsts of our own. First time to talk to God? First time to invite somebody to church? First time to exercise for better health? First time to quit smoking? Instances for firsts are endless! Important: Whatever "First" you do today, don't let it be the last...Keep it up, keep it up, you can do it again and again!

Today is Secret Saturday!

Today is SECRET SATURDAY! Do you have one? Most people do. Sometimes keeping a Secret either from choice or fear of hurting others is stressful. It's good to talk to someone about it, but you can't, can you! You can't divulge a secret. But *WAIT*! Yes, you *can*! First of all, you need to realize there IS someone who already knows your secrets. Every detail. Yep. The Heavenly Father knows every thought you've ever had from birth through now, as well as every movement you've ever made. Psalms 139:2 says, "*You know when I sit and when I rise; you perceive my thoughts from afar.*" How to handle this truth? Feel free to talk to Him about your secrets. About ANYthing. Your secret isn't new. He's heard it from millions through the ages with the same secret. Trust me. Trust Him! He'll help you with your secret. He'll work it out so you don't have to keep even one, or if you do, it's NO *Secret* that He'll give you peace about yours.

Today is Shepherd Sunday!

Today is SHEPHERD SUNDAY! My opinion is that one reason God loved David so much was because he was a good Shepherd, faithful to guide his sheep. Like the job He gave you; to watch over your family/flock. To guide and protect them. Then, David went to help in the fighting, slaying the giant Goliath. Just like you slay the giants who try to interfere with your family's peace. Then best for all of us is the Ultimate Shepherd, Jesus. Are you part of His flock? He'll leave the ninety-and-nine to come looking for you if you stray. Here are a few lines in a song I wrote: "*A small flock of sheep followed the Shepherd; the trail was rocky and steep. Each one had been sought, chosen and bought, and one of the small lambs was me. I watched as the Shepherd counted each sheep, making sure none had wandered astray; then He left all the flock to go searching for one missing lamb who fell by the way.*" Folks, if you stray, Jesus will come searching for you. Isn't that a comforting thought, that He loves us that much? Awesome Shepherd!

Week 2

Today is Mad Monday!

Today is MAD MONDAY! I am Mad at the devil. He has some of my friends and relatives fooled into complacency. He presents pretty ways and "things" that keep them from church. In Hebrews 10:25 God tells us that we should not forsake assembling ourselves together. What? Do we think the devil's gonna tempt us to stay out of church with something not fun? No! It'll be something we WANT to do more than we want to go to church. So, yeah, I'm MAD and I'm gonna do something about it! Gonna pray twice as hard that God will put a longing in the hearts of those friends and relatives, for *them* to line up with the Word and then...*they'll* get MAD at the devil, too. If more of us get our lives right and team up and get MAD at the enemy *together*, we'll make some progress in getting all of our friends and relatives headed on the journey to Heaven. We *do* want to go to Heaven, don't we? And we want our friends and relatives to go, too, don't we??? Well, let me see somebody getting *MAD,* then!

Today is Together Tuesday!

Today is TOGETHER TUESDAY! Together means "in contact with each other;" also "into agreement, harmony;" also "by combined action or effort." Do these describe our lives with our spouses, family, extended family, co-workers, church family, neighbors and community? And if not, then what about our individual moral and spiritual responsibility to do something about it? Together. *Together.* I said, Together!

Today is Weave Wednesday!

Today is WEAVE WEDNESDAY! (Interlacing, intertwining threads.) I wish every member of my family lived right around me. I think about our ancestors sometimes, wondering if they were all as closely knit as my family. At least they were pretty much able to live really close to each other in castles, etc., in those days. I have a sister who is the sibling that keeps all of our family "Weaved" together, since in today's world we live hundreds of miles from each other. She plans Reunions. She's right there when bad health hits any of us, etc. She weaves her love for us into a blanket of Caring, and we all feel it. Every family would be blessed to have a member like her. Perhaps you do. Perhaps your family is much like ours. None of my family members are perfect, me included, but our love is evident. Even on Facebook, etc., we're able to keep weaving that cloak of Love, so that it keeps us all under the same blanket called Family. Does your family need Weaving? Is there something you could do to help yours become closer and make your bond stronger? Our Heavenly Father is all about Family, too, so He will honor your efforts to make that happen and *help you* keep your family Weaving together. All you have to do is...give Him a chance to do that...

Today is Trophy Thursday!

Today is TROPHY THURSDAY! You know the little thrill you feel when you handle a situation right/make somebody happy/go the extra mile? Those are the trophies I'm talking about here. How many trophies can you win today? In 1 Samuel 15:22 God says, "*To obey is better than sacrifice*." Each time you obey Him and just "do right," another Trophy is awaiting you in Heaven. What a deal!

Today is Fleeting Friday!

Today is FLEETING FRIDAY! It started a few hours ago, and before you know it, it is half gone! Not much time left to do all the things we'd like to do in the few hours we're not asleep. So, we'd better act like the "Alvin" chipmunk song (Remember that one? If not, google ☺) and do things in high speed! Live (ultimately for God), love (your family/friends more), and laugh! (Go ahead, make those wrinkles.) Life is too Fleeting to stay in low gear very long, understand? Get ready...set...go!

Today is Surmount Saturday!

Today is SURMOUNT SATURDAY! (To excel, overcome.) Is there something you need to overcome? Maybe a fear of flying? I had to face that several years ago. I'll share my little story with you. My brother had his own plane, a two-seater. He flew into town and wanted to take us up for a short flight. My only son was six years old at the time and of course, begged to go up. My husband and I agreed to let him go, but I was praying the whole time for his safety. When they landed and taxied up beside us, my brother tried coaxing me into taking a turn, and he knew my fear of flying. I was protesting furiously, then all of a sudden it hit me (I know now it was the Holy Spirit speaking); how could I send my son into something I feared for myself, then not put myself into that same place!?! What kind of mother was I!?! So, I faced my fear right then, said yes, I'd go up, and you know? I had the *BEST* time! It was awesome! I surmounted my fear of flying, and may I say that I've Surmounted many different ones since. How? With God's help. ALWAYS. Got any fears? God will help you, too, to Surmount them.

Today is Sympathize Sunday!

Today is SYMPATHIZE SUNDAY! (To share in suffering.) Someone loses a loved one, another's house catches on fire, an acquaintance's car has gone its last mile, and you sympathize; but do you offer anything but clichés? Are your words "surface," and after you offer them, do you dismiss these troubles of others from your mind because you really "can't be bothered with anyone else's problems and you go about your own business, being glad that you make sure your life is not like that?" Bottom line, are there instances when/where you *could* be a little more sympathetic and say a sincere kind word – or even offer some help – rather than look down on their plight with your nose in the air? Hey, you may be walking in their shoes one of these days...you never know. We don't know the heartache or trial a person is dealing with, so take your hand, raise it to your face, and pull your nose out of the air...Yes, that looks better now.

Week 3

Today is Meritable Monday!

Today is MERITABLE MONDAY! (The fact of deserving well – or ill.) Do you get accolades from your family for the way you conduct yourself around them? After all, they're the ones you're supposed to be impressing, guiding, etc. Example: What about your driving attitude? Your teens learning how to drive are sure to have watched you through the years. Are you courteous? Aware of drivers and scenarios around you? That's good. There *are* some drivers who get in the passing lane and won't speed up to get in front of the semi beside them – or won't slow down to get behind it – and out of the way of drivers lined up behind them. Apparently, they don't realize that maybe someone in that passing lane is trying to get to another state where their loved one is in the hospital near death. If you're a good role model by courteously driving in the lane you're supposed to be in, let me say that I respect you, Meritable Person! Thanks for looking out for other folks!

Today is Tardy Tuesday!

Today is TARDY TUESDAY. Oh, the times in my life I've been late for this or that; always having to give explanations, reasons why, plus apologies. Late for dental appointments (Didn't want to go in the first place ☺, hate that drill...!), late meeting friends for lunch (Well, you wouldn't want to be on time and shock them now, would you!), late for Sunday School, etc. All of that's okay, life will still go on, but guess what...There is *no* arriving late when Jesus comes back to take His Family home to Heaven. Either you're ready for that "twinkling of an eye" event or you'll be left behind. And you won't like that kind of tardy! Train yourself to be a better steward of your time. It'll be fun being early...instead of Tardy.

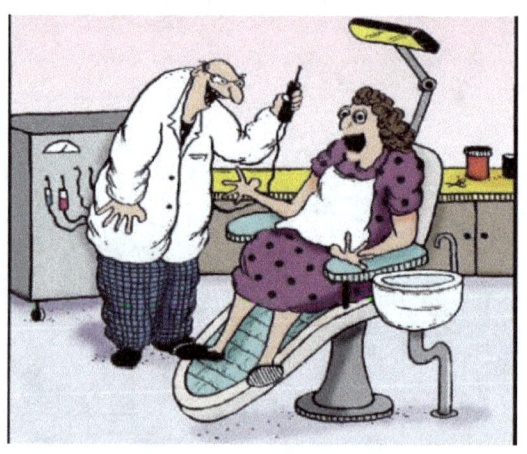

Today is Wallow Wednesday!

Today is WALLOW WEDNESDAY! Meaning: "To indulge oneself immoderately." Some folks wallow in luxury. You can actually wallow in happiness. Various things to wallow in. Pigs love to wallow in mud. It's ok to wallow, just be careful what you're wallowing in....There are always consequences to everything you do. Consider them before you choose what to wallow in. Mud only? Will wash off ☺. Some other stains or consequences won't. Hey, *you* there! What are you thinking about Wallowing in ☺?

Today is Trove Thursday!

Today is TROVE THURSDAY! (A store of valuable or delightful things.) If you're a man and let's say a friend from your college days comes to visit, you'll want to show him your Trove of "Toys," and talk about your special accomplishments. Same with the ladies; you'll be showing off your children, their "cuteness," your beautiful home, your china, pictures of your life since college, etc. Consider this: Your *Mind* is a Trove. It really is. It holds "Sweet Nothings." It holds knowledge of favorite things your spouse just loves. Do you use the "Sweet Nothings" on your Sweetie? Do you use your Trove of knowledge to come up with ideas to *show* your love for him/her, just like you practiced when you were dating? The mind, *your* mind, is an awesome thing. God created it to be just that. Let's use it more to GIVE OUT the Trove of good things to others. Just think on this, okay? Today can start a "new day" for yourself, giving out Treasures from your Trove! (Don't forget to give *back* to Him what He gave to YOU!)

Today is Fascinating Friday!

Today is FASCINATING FRIDAY! "And why?" you ask. Because with the awful shape the world is in right now, I'm Fascinated that God has allowed us to see the sun rise on this very day. Isn't it fascinating? Keeps us warm at times, gives us light, plus helps with good health. I'm also fascinated that God had His Master Plan in the beginning for the universe, and that includes you and me...Ever wonder why He put you in today's world – instead of perhaps the 1100s or before??? What part of His plan are YOU working on?

Today is Spectacular Saturday!

Today is SPECTACULAR SATURDAY! Today...can be Spectacular for you. "Really? How?" you say. You're just gonna be driving to work, then you'll be inside a building. Nah, not spectacular, you think. Well, *I'm* saying it *can* be. But it's up to you to make it that way. Can be a regular ol' day, or a spectacular one! Simply according to how you look at it! See that beautiful tree you just passed? That was the Great I Am, Creator of all mankind, animals, zillions of stars, and *God's* face you just saw! *Pretty spectacular*! That vehicle you're driving? A total product of men's minds – using the knowledge God gave them – for you to be able to scoot to work in comfort instead of riding a horse all the way. Even that pen you're writing with at work? That water cooler? That phone? Well, you get the idea for the word. It's Spectacular. All of it. Because the same One that engineered all of that...created *YOU*! And *you're* the most Spectacular thing in your day that God created! Get used to it. Repeat after me; I am Spectacular! I am Spectacular! I am Spectacular! I AM SPECTACULAR!!! (Okay, okay, don't get the big-head ☺!)

Today is Strengthen Sunday!

Today is STRENGTHEN SUNDAY! Scriptures say, "*The Lord's Strength is made perfect in our weakness.*" Awesome! Also, "*I can do all things through Christ which strengthens me.*" What wonderful Scriptures!!! "All" things, it says. Not just some of them. And, through Christ. Don't ever leave Him out of anything you do. If you do, you'll fall flat on your face. Some of us have already learned that ☺.

Week 4

Today
is
More Monday!

Today is MORE MONDAY! Let's use this word we all know so well. Eat More? No, not in quantity, but yes, more healthy foods! Read more Bible? Yes! Great instructions for daily living in there! Make more attempts to be a better citizen, to witness about Jesus, to educate yourself on the world situation, pray more, give more, help more, more—more—more this Monday? Yes, yes, yes! Don't stop today. Continue it…More!

Today is Tarry Tuesday!

Today is TARRY TUESDAY! Means "Delay. Linger. Abide in a place." I'm not pleased with myself when I mostly pray "on the run." Now and then after I read some in the Bible, then pray, I say, "Okay Life, wait up! Gotta take time to linger in that Special Place with my Lord!" Feels sooooooooooo good! Only thing is – I don't do that near as much as I need/want to. How about you, my Friend?

Today is Watermelon Wednesday!

Today is WATERMELON WEDNESDAY! We say, "*Life is a bowl of cherries,*" but folks, wait until the Watermelon bursts ☺! I walked into my kitchen to get something behind the watermelon on my counter that I'd bought only three days before and when I turned it to one side just a bit, it burst like a balloon filled with liquid watermelon! Juice went EVERYwhere. I was standing there wailing ☺, thinking it was surely going to take *all* afternoon to clean everything up and I had SO much to do already without this happening! Might as well get started, I thought. Cleared the counter of all objects. Put a garbage bag on the floor and even as I tried to ease the watermelon down into it, it was like a soft pliable rubber ball. Took it to the garbage can outside. Soaked up the floor with two big towels, plus two for the counter. Put them in the Washer. Disinfected the counter, mopped the floor, put the appliances back in place and voila! I'd finished the whole job in twenty minutes! A miracle! Isn't that just how God handles *our* "Watermelon bursts?" Something unexpected happens and looks daunting to us, but He makes it all disappear quickly. Yay God! Have you had any Watermelon Wednesdays ☺?

Today is Tremendous Thursday!

Today is TREMENDOUS THURSDAY! Means "extremely good or impressive; excellent." As teens we think our future will always show Tremendous results. From the time we get our drivers' license, take that first step into college, or say, "I do" to our sweetheart and head into life, it's all tremendous (Just ask *me* ☺). What about when you just asked Jesus into your heart/life? Wasn't that Tremendous?!? Actually, it will be the most Tremendous event you've ever been involved in! You'll have many more Tremendous blessings heaped on you on your journey in Life, but just wait until you get to Heaven...Treeee*mendous*!

Today is Finish Friday!

Today is FINISH FRIDAY. How many little jobs/projects have you started and not Finished? You may not have procrastinated; you may have just gotten interrupted or you ran out of time for the day, etc., and never got back to it. Sometimes those things can make you lose interest as well as your initial excitement for what you were doing, and that may hamper your desire to get back to it. Your projects could range from painting to finishing a particular chapter in the Bible. Resolve today to finish at least *one* job that got laid aside. When you Finish, you'll feel like a new person. Just do it!

Today is Shipshape Saturday!

Today is SHIPSHAPE SATURDAY! Get your Ship in Shape to sail the oceans of life because there will be some stormy weather along the way. Build AND repair your ship with safety instructions from God's Word, the Bible. You'll find there'll be repairs after repairs on your journey, so keep those instructions close. Captain Jesus will be your pilot! What about it!?! Can't do better than that, can you!

Today is Shoulder Sunday!

Today is SHOULDER SUNDAY! Our Lord's Shoulder is always there to lean on, and what a shoulder! Go ahead...lean. He's watching you, knows you need to lean, just waiting on you, hoping you do, so He can shoulder your load. For those who don't need to lean right now...somebody out there needs *YOUR* Shoulder...

Week 5

Today is Manna Monday!

Today is MANNA MONDAY! If you don't know what Manna is, go to the Bible concordance and look it up. (Or google it ☺.) God has fed manna to me all day long all the days of my life! I wake up breathing, first manna. Limbs moving, another meal. Thinking for myself, another. Great phone call from a friend, another helping. List goes on and on. I look forward to all the manna I'll be blessed with again and again! What kind of Manna will you be partaking of today???

Today is There Tuesday!

Today is THERE TUESDAY! "There where?" you say. To the place you've been heading, that's where! Whether it's a financial focus/goal, emotional, a health goal, or most important – a spiritual goal, it's a win/win situation if you don't falter or give up. You can do it! How? By not trying to do it by yourself. Three words are so comforting; "In God's Strength" we can do anything! So, keep progressing, and get "There."

Today is Write Wednesday!

Today is WRITE WEDNESDAY! We don't visit like our Grandparents did in their day. We don't even send letters in the mail like we used to. We do write, though. Email, Facebook, etc. Feels good to keep in touch with friends and relatives, plus meet new friends, too. Sometimes we can put words into a letter that we can't say in person. Ever thought about writing a letter to God? If you do, get ready for the deep things to come out of your heart, because once you start, it's amazing what all you'll want to say to Him! I can assure you that He'll absolutely LOVE it if you Write to Him!

Today is Tidy Thursday!

Today is TIDY THURSDAY! We go through our homes to Tidy up the mess we've made. Vacuum up the dust that's settled. Take out the trash. Today is a good time to tidy our minds, bodies and souls. Straighten up Life's priorities. Take out the things that are not good for our lives, not to mention our eternal well-being! After we've finished – just like when we vacuum our floors – see how clean we are? Not messy anymore. Tidy. Good feeling.

Today is Fireball Friday!

Today is FIREBALL FRIDAY! From the time we all arise we're usually rushing "to and fro" furiously. Accomplishing. Focusing. Finishing up the week's unfinished things. Wonder what our lives would be like if we did this for Our Creator...Don't you know that He would bless us beyond measure??? Being a Fireball for Him would probably be akin to the passion we felt for Jesus when we were first Saved, feeling like we were on fire for Him. How long has it been since you felt that? (Just asking...)

Today is Shirker Saturday!

Today is SHIRKER SATURDAY! (To avoid an obligation.) Are you a Shirker? I sure hope not! Shame on you if you are! As a human, you have an obligation to your soul/life. (1) Don't send yourself to Hell and (2) Men, you're the spiritual head of your household (Bible said that, not me)! It's up to you to guide your family to Heaven. To the world's population: Help each other...Fulfill obligations! Don't be a Shirker!!!

Today is Stupendous Sunday!

Today is STUPENDOUS SUNDAY! (Causing astonishment or wonder.) The biggest wonder ever known to man is that we can live forever...and forever...and forever. No end to living. That's so hard to even imagine, because to man, everything has an end here on this earth. But it's true! Not only do we live forever, it's in a place of Paradise! Jesus made this possible for us. Ever heard of Him? If not, you'll find Him in a book called the Bible. Turn to the books of Matthew, Mark, Luke and John, and you can "meet" Him there. Just meeting Him is stupendous! He performed many wonders while He lived here on this earth! Multitudes were astonished at His works! After you meet Him, you can make plans to live with Him in Heaven. Now, *there's* a place that's Stupendous! I'm going there, are you?

Week 6

Today is Milestone Monday!

Today is MILESTONE MONDAY! Means "A significant point in development." Sometimes on Mondays we're not as sharp as other days. Recovering from lazy weekends. Good reason to change that. Make Mondays important, too! Something you've procrastinated on? "Milestone it" today! Choose to do better on something negative in your life, then choose someone to hold you accountable until you've conquered it. It could be a friend, a Church-Family member, a relative, or even your Heavenly Father…

Today is Treasure Tuesday!

Today is TREASURE TUESDAY. I found the Treasure! I did! I found it! You hadn't heard about the biggest treasure that exists? It's Jesus...God's Son! *He's* the Treasure! Yes, *Jesus*! All you have to do is invite Him into your heart and life and He'll take you to His home in Heaven, which will be your new home and it's *full* of treasures! A fabulous mansion all your own, streets of gold; the riches go on and on, and you'll live there *FOREVER*! So glad I found the treasure! There's a map (Bible) with clues (John 3:16) for you. What. A. Treasure!

Today is Withstand Wednesday!

Today is WITHSTAND WEDNESDAY! (Defined as: To oppose with firm determination.) When my husband was in his thirties, he found himself involved in a Strike where he worked. There he was on the corner of Third and Monroe in Memphis, Tennessee, holding a Strike sign, while his ten-year old son, Monty, was at home fighting cancer. Here are his words: "The devil got on my shoulder and said, 'Ray Lewis, you're a fool. God doesn't love you. Look at your life. Your car is falling apart from driving so many miles singing and preaching for the Lord, you don't know if your son will be alive when you get home, and now your job is gone.'" Ray said, all of a sudden, he sensed the Lord on his other shoulder and began to remind him of all the blessings he'd received through the years. He said, "The devil had to leave and I put that sign down and wrote three songs." The rest of the story? Connie Smith (Grand Ole Opry Star) recorded two of those songs! (One, "I'd Still Want to Serve Him" says, "*If God should ordain that Heaven should vanish, I'd still want to serve Him because of all He's already done for me.*") God blessed Ray just because he allowed God to help him withstand the devil's lies. Folks, don't give the devil an inch! Withstand! If Ray can do it, *you* can!

Today is Tolerant Thursday!

Today is TOLERANT THURSDAY! I could mention many things in all our lives that we COULD be more tolerant about, but no time/space for much. One instance, maybe you're showing the new employee how to do work that's not familiar to them. As each hour passes today, see how many actions you can work on – being more Tolerant...Always remember, you don't have to do it on your own; the God of ALL is there to assist/guide. Isn't that wonderful?!?!

Today is Forgotten Friday!

Today is FORGOTTEN FRIDAY! Have you Forgotten to do something for someone? Something you promised to do? On the receiving end of that, I can tell you it hurts to suspect you've just been plain forgotten. Makes you feel like you don't matter. Been there more than once. I often think of ol' Daniel and admire that he prayed THREE times a day, and I think, "I wonder how he always remembered to do that!" Never forgot, according to the Bible. Wonder how Jesus feels when we forget *Him*!?! In Heaven, He's worshipped. But here on earth, though He keeps knocking on our doors patiently, He's aware that He's been "Forgotten." Especially in our daily lives. When we have a crisis in our lives, we're quick to remember Him, though, aren't we! He must *really* love us to put up with our forgetting to even talk to Him, except on Sundays! Have you Forgotten Jesus?

Today is Simple Saturday!

Today is SIMPLE SATURDAY! Simple means free from complexity. Simple things in life are all we actually NEED for the mind, body, and soul. An overload of Life's clutter can harm the mind. Overload of food ditto on the body. Soul? Too many folks think being a Christian is complex. Not so. Our pastor says about the Bible, "Read it...and do it!" Now, how Simple is that?!?

Today is Serve Sunday!

Today is SERVE SUNDAY. Who do *you* Serve? Are you one that pays attention mostly to "me, me, me," and everything's "I this" or "I that?" Or, are you one that is always aware of others around you that you can help in some way!?!? Some folks serve at church services in different capacities; that's needed and commendable. But in your day-to-day workplace environment, *service to others is a service to the Lord.* If you're serving others with a servant's heart, *sounds* like you're serving Jesus. Now, *that's* The One you want to Serve!!!

Week 7

Today is Marvelous Monday!

Today is MARVELOUS MONDAY! (Causing wonder; astonishing.) I mean for it to be Marvelous this whole day! For one thing, I can never quit being thankful that my Creator put me in this day and age where we have so many push-button conveniences of life to help us with chores. From the laundry room to the home office computers/printers/tablets, etc., we live in a great Time! If my computer is slow for whatever reason and I become aggravated, I've made it a habit to place myself – in my mind's eye – in the 1800s when there were no computers. That brings me to my senses and gives me the patience I need to get through that moment. It's so marvelous to live in this stage of Time! It's especially marvelous to know that when Life for me is over on earth, I am going to an even *more* marvelous place! 1 Corinthians 2:9 says, "*Eye hath not seen, nor ear heard, neither have entered into the heart of man, the things which God hath prepared for them that love Him.*" Are you going to this Marvelous place? Great! I'll see you there!

Today is Topnotch Tuesday!

Today is TOPNOTCH TUESDAY! Not in the dictionary, but used when we score, set records, or make our mark in situations. That's what "notch" means, and we all know what TOP means. All days are great for me, even when I shed tears from sorrow about a loved one going to Heaven, because by Conscious Choice I turned them into tears of joy that they've "made it!" Each day, folks, can be Topnotch in sooooo many ways! If you don't believe that, make yourself a list of good versus bad! You'll see!

Today is Whoopee Wednesday!

Today is WHOOPEE WEDNESDAY! Most mid-week church services are on Wednesday night as we meet to worship God together. I think it's so great when you start thinking about the coming service a few hours before time to walk in the door of your church. You may only be thinking about what you're going to wear, the members of your Church-Family that you'll be glad to see, or what songs will be sung. But you're thinking about church, and going there to praise God is a "given." Nothing like a Church-Family worshipping God together. I said God. The only God. There is no other, never has been, never will be. End of subject, except let me say a big "Whoopee" because it's exciting to be able to do all of this! But hey, don't wait until tonight to worship God. Start right now! Heaven will surely be worshipping with you...And you know what I have to say about that? WHOOPEE ☺!

Today is Team Thursday!

Today is TEAM THURSDAY! Once when my daughter, granddaughter and grandson were visiting, we began doing a little project together. Granddaughter said with a note of pride, "We're a team, aren't we...!" How proud I was of her; she was only a pre-teen. All families should be a team. All co-workers should be a team. All church members should be a team. All Christians world-wide should be a team. Striving for the same end result, helping each other every day! Dictionary says "to yoke or join." What Team are *YOU* helping???

Today is Fair Friday!

Today is FAIR FRIDAY! Definition I'm talking about is "just." Are you Fair to all folks around you? About the only thing that *really* makes me mad in life is "UNfairness." When I see others doing or saying things that are unfair, I see "red!" I hope you're not an unfair person. Most fair of all? God, obviously. What a fair/just God! Blesses us when we don't even deserve it...Fair thing to do is at least thank Him for it! So, have yourself a Fair Friday, how 'bout it!

Today is Striking Saturday!

Today is STRIKING SATURDAY! After realizing how pure God's love is for us all, and that He took time to create each one of us uniquely, when I look into the face of one stranger or a hundred, I see how striking they look! Striking how God gave each of us our own personal eyebrows, lips, nose, cheekbone structure, etc. Go, quick! Look in the mirror! A striking reflection will look back at you! So, strut today because you're a Striking individual that God Himself created!

Today is Symphony Sunday!

Today is SYMPHONY SUNDAY! One definition of Symphony is "harmony of any kind." Definition of harmony? "Agreement in..." My marriage has been a symphony, PTL! Hope yours is. What about being in harmony with God? Our lives being in tune with Him definitely makes a symphony! I get so happy with Life; my cup just runs over and I "hear" a Symphony in my heart! I wish for all...a Symphony of Life!

Week 8

Today is Miracle Monday!

Today is MIRACLE MONDAY! You awake? A miracle! You could've died during the night. Able to move to get out of bed? A miracle. Out of bed by yourself? A double miracle. Many cannot manage that without help. Can you talk? Another miracle. Are you blind? No? Another miracle! Are you deaf? No? Wow, yet another one. Are you cognitive enough to drive? Great! Drive to a job? Awesome! A life just packed full of *miracles*! There are tens of thousands of folks alive right now on this earth that would give anything to have just *some* of your miracles, and you have a day already filled with them! If you watch through the whole day, you'll be able to see a lot more miracles in your life. You see, there are no small miracles. A miracle is a miracle. Be aware of the many around you. Today is YOUR Miracle Monday!

Today is Tiller Tuesday!

Today is TILLER TUESDAY! (Till is to work by sowing or cultivating.) Most "practicing" Christians will tell you they believe the End of Time here on Earth is about to arrive. "So," some have been heard to say, "Why should I work as hard as I have been for the Kingdom?" My opinion for that is a scripture in the Bible (Luke 19:13) that directs us to "*Occupy till He comes.*" That means to continue our jobs for the Lord as usual till the end. I personally plan to till (write and sing) until He says my work is finished and calls me Home. Plus, I'll do it with joy in my heart! A Tiller is special to the Lord. We all need to keep tilling the ground and reap the harvest for the Kingdom. How often do *you* till, Tiller?

Today is Warrior Wednesday!

Today is WARRIOR WEDNESDAY! Yesteryear's definition is "A brave or experienced soldier or fighter; engaged in warfare." Today's definition says, "A person who is very strong and doesn't give up easily." (For instance, "He battled cancer like a warrior.") Usually our days give us a battle of one kind or another, and that's why we need to learn to lean on God's Word to help us through "stuff." Personally, I don't mind telling you, I am a Warrior! I am not a weenie! (Unless I'm faced with a big ol' black bear ☺.) My choice! I refuse to not live life to the fullest, and I can only do that by depending on my God. I tell Him that I know I can't even walk without Him beside me, holding my hand. Folks, that's *how* I can be a Warrior. Holding to God's Hand. Best feeling in the world!

Today is Transmission Thursday!

Today is TRANSMISSION THURSDAY! Meaning: "The gears by which the power is Transmitted from the engine of an automobile to the axel (or wheels) that propels the vehicle." Let's parallel that to our own lives. Ther it would read, "The measure of your efforts, by which your plan, focus, and determination is sent from the mind of YOU to your limbs/mouth/action that accomplishes what you decided to do." Maybe do something unusual for needy folks? Start a new work in your church? And will your Transmission be set in Low...or High gear...?

Today is Funny Friday!

Today is FUNNY FRIDAY! Why is it Funny? Because I've *chosen* to make it funny ☺. Too many serious things in life not to have funny days! So, maybe you can make today a funny one for yourself, too! See how many situations you can make funny...It'll be...Funny making that happen...!

Today is Silly Saturday!

Today is SILLY SATURDAY, since yesterday was Funny Friday! Let's stay in that same groove a while. Feels good to just lighten up, doesn't it! We all – especially in today's world – have way too many serious matters to deal with, so we need to take every chance we have to be funny and silly. Being silly is okay, too! If someone looks at you sideways, just say, "This is my Silly time!" (Way to go, you're doing it ☺!)

Today is Shower Sunday!

Today is SHOWER SUNDAY! Christians rejoice about God's "Showers" of Blessings. He loves us, so why would He not want to shower us with them. And we surely need, want and love those blessings! However, today *let's turn that around*...Let's shower *God* with blessings! You can figure how to do that on your own, I know. Keep score; don't take this lightly! At the end of the day, see if God had to get an umbrella because our blessings were Showering Him so heavily!!!

Week 9

Today is Moving Monday!

Today is MOVING MONDAY! Many of us travel from city to city or state to state with the jobs that we have, and I'm one of those. Today I'm moving from one place/state/town and situation to the other, but as I'm moving, I'm taking The Good Lord with me!!! He's with me every step and every mile. I've heard so many folks tell me that one of their favorite places to pray is while they're in their vehicle. Me too, me too! (And we surely need to pray for safety while we're in today's traffic ☺, don't we, folks!) Sooooooooooooo comforting to have the Creator of the Universe with me, right there in the front seat of my car, Moving right along with me! Isn't that awesome!?

Today is Thrive Tuesday!

Today is THRIVE TUESDAY! One definition is to grow vigorously. Let your mind go back down Memory Lane in your life, adolescent to teen to adult...Perception of Life grew. *Then* what? *Mature, stable, functional* adult handling Life's Curves correctly is Thriving. A victory! While thriving emotionally, thrive spiritually too, okay? Milk to meat. Do it daily. You'll see a Thriving in your whole life that can't be surpassed!

Today is Wait Wednesday!

Today is WAIT WEDNESDAY! Hard to Wait, cause we're human, but just Wait upon the Lord and all will work out. Mere words you say? Try it. To try means you'll have to trust Him implicitly. Can you? Have you ever? Now daily stuff that we contend with; waiting on obnoxious drivers that won't get out of the passing lane, waiting anxiously in line to use the bathroom, holding your tongue before it lashes out in a remark you can't take back...waiting, hoping your conscience will tell you not eat that fattening thing. (Just ask the Lord to take the calories out ☺.) WAIT on the Lord and have a great day, Everyone!

Today is Tend Thursday!

Today is TEND THURSDAY! Tend means pay attention to, serve, care for. Your job, your business matters, family, friends, pets, finances, vehicle upkeep, all of it. How you tend shows your character. Did you know that? Most importantly, what about your salvation? Do you give it any attention? God tells us in 2 Timothy 2:15 to "*Study, to shew thyself approved unto God.*" Meaning the Bible. Read it...and do it...then better character evolves. You're "Tending."

Today is Family Friday!

Today is FAMILY FRIDAY! Some of my children live in states other than mine and I don't get to see them often. When I'm able to spend time with family, it's one of the blessings for which I've been so grateful. Makes me think of the Family of God. Is there a member of your family or the Family of God that you just don't "like?" Let me share how to get past that. Just look at that person "through God's eyes" and you will have to feel differently about him/her. It'll teach you how to love all of God's Family. His Master Plan has always been about The Family. I'm so tickled to be part of His Family, aren't you??

Today is Storm Saturday!

Today is STORM SATURDAY. It's gonna Storm. You can count on it. Not always a nice rain-pelting-on-the-roof storm. Sometimes they'll be full of high winds that'll try to knock your house down. But, don't stress; Jesus knows all about storms and He can say, "Peace, be still" and the storm in your life will calm. Stand firm in your journey through Life, make sure your home (faith) is built on the Rock and not on the sand, and not only will you come through the storm okay, you'll see that sweet sun open up from the Heavens to shine Peace on you! Storms. Scary? Nah. Not when you're walking through them with your hand in the Lord's.

Today is Shake Sunday!

Today is SHAKE SUNDAY! Now and then God will Shake our world up; well, doesn't He *have* to from time to time – in order to get our attention??? We pay him no or little attention most of the time. So, does He need to Shake *you*? Surely hope not! He had to Shake me a time or two in my life and it wasn't fun…!

Week 10

Today is Major Monday!

Today is MAJOR MONDAY! Today is a great place in the week for making Major decisions. Like who to help. Who to bless? What to give. What to accomplish; opportunities are limitless on these things. What we perceive to be small decisions to help others are major in God's eyes, and He's the Bookkeeper, so He oughta know ☺. Many times, though, we're too caught up in our own troubles to help others. Chorus in a song my sweet husband wrote; *"Reach out and touch somebody as you walk along Life's Road; sometimes a word or a friendly smile will lift a heavy load; you'll feel so much better knowing that you've helped, and who knows, someday you may need a little help yourself...."* Have a grand "Major" Monday!

Today is Talk Tuesday!

Today is TALK TUESDAY!!! Have you ever just "Talked" to God? It's incredible! He listens...Talk to Him. Communication is verrrrry important in any relationship. Do you talk to your spouse? NOT talking is to not communicate. Listen to me: "*Folks can deal with what they know; they can't deal with what they don't know.*" (That's from me, Laura, Chapter 7, Verse 1 ☺.) Talking heals. Let me repeat that...Talking heals.

Today is Wise Wednesday!

Today is WISE WEDNESDAY. Dictionary says "To become informed or knowledgeable." Wise. I like that word. King Solomon is known for being the wisest man known, throughout the Bible, anyway. I have tried to make wiser decisions year after year as I have traveled this journey called Life. I'm not always successful at it, but learning lessons from making mistakes can make you wiser. Maybe you venture to become wiser with each birthday, too. We all could probably exercise more wisdom in *some* areas. Sometimes the little daily things are the ones that we need to "wise up" on the most...I find I'm still "wising up" every day that I live ☺. Do you have things you need to be Wiser about? Just asking...

Today is Tall Thursday!

Today is TALL THURSDAY! "Tall?" you say. "What does that have to do with a day?" Hang on, I'll tell you...Tall means "High in stature." Stature means development; growth. One of my daughters said my grandson (age 14) is six feet tall already, but I'll tell you what's taller than his six-foot height...His heart! Has respect/compassion/love for elders, mentally challenged, etc. Regular teen; he hunts, fishes, rides sports vehicles, etc. All "guy." All heart. Room to add more great qualities. What about it? For your age, how Tall are you?

Today is Forward Friday!

Today is FORWARD FRIDAY! No need for a definition, you know what it means. For crying out loud (or "weeping noisily," as one daughter laughingly says), why would you want to go backwards? Oh, I know we ladies would like our faces to go back to when we didn't have so many wrinkles ☺, but most will confess they wouldn't want to go "backwards." Just think of how our Pioneer ancestors – with their vision of settling the West – yelled, "Forward, Ho!" each morning as their wagon trains took them a few more miles. Surely today we can follow in their footsteps and go Forward in our endeavors! What great determination they had! What perseverance! A Christian's vision should be Heaven, and we should always go forward each day to meet Jesus there. He surely went forward – for us – up Calvary's Hill, didn't He! A verse I wrote; *"God promised no roses on the Road to Gloryland, but the roses will come later when we shake that nail-scarred hand. So, when things close in around you, keep going on, don't give up, for where would we be if Jesus had said, 'It's too much.'"* So glad He kept walking Forward, aren't you!?!

Today is Suitable Saturday!

Today is SUITABLE SATURDAY! (Adapted to a use, satisfying, able, qualified.) I once heard a minister say that usually everyone has a set of "rules" by which we personally judge everyone else. That's probably as true a statement as anything else I've heard. Sometimes we look at folks who are less fortunate than we are and we delegate them to a lower level than we've placed ourselves. However, aren't we glad that God says all men are equal! He's talking about our souls. From a drunk in the gutter to the richest man in the world, we're all Suitable to ask Jesus to forgive us for our sins, accept Him into our hearts, then travel towards Heaven! We're all eligible. We all qualify! Again, everyone, from Adam and Eve to the most-evil criminal that's ever lived...qualifies. They're suitable to drop on their knees and meet Jesus. Whether they will or not...that's up to them. Choices. That's sooooooo what Life's about. What will *you* choose, Suitable Person?

Today is Selective Sunday!

Today is SELECTIVE SUNDAY! Consequences in everything we do/say, we all know that by now. If we can make it a HABIT to think before we speak/act – and be *Selective* in that – not only can we make someone else's day, we'll feel a whole lot better about ourselves! Selective in friends, reading material, music, well, you get the picture. What about – Select Sunday to spend more time with the Lord! He'd *LOVE* that!

Week 11

Today is Millionaire Monday!

Today is MILLIONAIRE MONDAY! How can you tell me I'm a Millionaire when I eat "peas and taters" all the time? Well, here it is: You may have to eat cornbread and peas a lot of the time, and you may only have a dollar to your name, but as long as you have Jesus in your heart, *you're a MILLIONAIRE!* And do you know what else? You already have a mansion built for you in Heaven! Not only that, you have a robe and crown waiting on you! So, "Welcome Mr., Mrs., Ms. or Miss Millionaire," to Millionaire Monday!

Today is Tickled Tuesday!

Today is TICKLED TUESDAY. No, nobody Tickled me in the ribs ☺ but I've noticed that I'm still alive and breathing, so that makes me glad; tickles me! God is good! Somebody in the world is aggravated right now about something, but all is well in your world, so that should tickle you. Now: Why not tickle somebody else! No, not in the ribs, you silly-willy person ☺, tickle their attitude by passing on your appreciation of the very opportunity you have...to be Tickled!

Today is Wean Wednesday!

Today is WEAN WEDNESDAY! Meaning of Wean? "To detach from a cause of dependence." Wow, that covers a multitude of habits. Let your mind wander, then pray HARD for the ones you know you have that could be termed as dependent. We were all weaned from the bottle as babies – by someone else. Now, as an adult, we surely can Wean ourselves! Or………are we weaker than a baby...Whaddaya think ☺?

Today is Tone Thursday!

Today is TONE THURSDAY! Style or manner of expression...Tones say more than words. We've all heard "It's the way they said it that hurt." After being married to your spouse for years, same words you said then, now are said with a different tone. Practice better tones on your spouse and it will carry over to everybody else ☺...You can change from a Sergeant to a Sweetie ☺...when you change your Tone!

Today is Friendly Friday!

Today is FRIENDLY FRIDAY! I hate picking up the phone to find it's a telemarketer, don't you? I have my answers ready, and they aren't Friendly! Wonder how many people do that same thing. So, I have to change that, because surely telemarketers need a friendly voice now and then! After all, they have to make a living, too, just like we do. I can say, "No," but still be friendly/cheerful as I say it. Wish them a blessed day! How about it, folks, can we be Friendlier?

Today is Stage Saturday!

Today is STAGE SATURDAY! When you give your heart and life to Jesus Christ, *right then* you walk on to a "Stage." A stage where everybody in your world will be watching your Christian "walk." Don't just "talk the talk; *WALK* the talk!" And it is *your* stage. You're the Star! You can make such a difference in lives around you. You see, because you're God's Star, you're a God-Rep! You represent Him! So, in any situation you meet within your daily movements, before you're required to respond to anything, make it a habit to say to yourself, "What would Coach Jesus do?" Your "Acting Coach" is ready to help you with your "lines!" Be the Star that God wants you to be on your stage! Your actions, your joy, your attitude, all of it can entice someone else to join you on that stage. The aim is to get as many folks as we can to stand on God's Stage...before the end of time.

Today is Star Sunday!

Today is STAR SUNDAY! We've talked about you being on stage as one of God's Stars, now who's the number one Star in *your* life? Some would name their spouse, their children, parents, etc., and that's understandable. However, our Lord Jesus Christ – the most famous name for over two-thousand years – should be your favorite Star. Why? Because – for goodness sakes – He gave His life, His beaten and crucified body, so that *you* could have the opportunity to even *choose* your favorite Star! Hey Everybody, today let's all say, "Today is Star Sunday and Jesus is my Star!"

Week 12

Today is Monotony Monday!

Today is MONOTONY MONDAY! (Tedious repetition and routine.) Is your life full of Monotony? Break it! There are different things to help. If you're "on the job," pray silently for different relatives and friends that need it. Sing hymns that you know, even in your mind. Do multiplications ☺. When you are off work, DO something different besides watch TV. Go! Go and do *what* you think. Here's some ideas: Cruise the countryside, making pictures with your phone-camera, of old barns, pretty mountain scenes, creeks, cattle grazing, etc. Then go to a Nursing Home. Tell them you want to bring "the outside" to an older person who can't get out to see it. They'll know exactly who needs that. This will make someone's day! Another thing to break the monotony in your life: Locate a cemetery. Get permission, then using a flat-head screwdriver, scrape out the dirt around the markings, making them easier to read. (There are older headstones where time and erosion has made the markings hard to read.) There are many little jobs like these which will add substance to your life, help others, and...say "Goodbye" to Monotony.

Today is Technique Tuesday!

Today is TECHNIQUE TUESDAY! Means "method of procedure that produces skill in any profession." For instance, if you're a Christian determined to witness about Jesus to someone, your technique (way you go about it) is important. You want to witness, not offend. Also, the technique you use in anything from seeking employment to cooking could make a difference. Take care. Work on your Technique...and *it'll* work for *you*!

Today is Whiz Wednesday!

Today is WHIZ WEDNESDAY! To whir (Go swiftly) or hum like a speeding bullet. Like me when I grab my duster, mop, or the vacuum ☺. One of my daughters likes to whiz to church. (Our church is a very exciting place to attend. It's a "Word" church. A "family.") Years ago, she said to me, "Mom, if folks can't feel anticipation by 1 P.M. on Wednesday about church that night, they need to find another church ☺. Lots of truth in that. Do you Whiz to church...or go from duty?

Today is Tribute Thursday!

Today is TRIBUTE THURSDAY! (Something given voluntarily as deserved.) I'd like to give Tribute to a few guys that may never read this. A few years ago, Lewis & Lewis were starting on a tour and stopped between Nashville and Memphis to get something cold to drink. A sight met our eyes that has been forever in my heart. Several motorcycles were parked on the side of the parking lot of that convenience store, and guys were standing beside them in a circle with their arms locked around the shoulders of the one next to them. Their heads were bowed and they were praying! Unashamedly! Right there in the parking lot, not caring who saw them. I was soooo proud of them, and I said a quick "Hallelujah" praise to Heaven for them! We don't see much prayer in public nowadays. So, you motorcycle guys? Whoever and wherever you are – and God knows that – I give you Tribute! God bless each one of you for Standing for Him! Luke 9:26 says, "*For whosoever shall be ashamed of me and of my words, of him shall...*" (Hey, go look it up and read the rest of it for yourself. See what will happen if you're ashamed of Jesus.)

Today is Flaw Friday!

Today is FLAW FRIDAY! (An often-hidden defect, a faulty part, weakness in something.) Hey. We're all full of them. Try to keep them hidden, though, don't we! And you know we're not talking about physical flaws here ☺. But knowing what you know, you *know* your Heavenly Father knows about *every one* of them. Still loves you anyway in spite of imperfections that have become part of you. Maybe you're too hasty with sarcasm (good example) or frown at folks when there's no need, etc. But, since this is Flaw Friday, why not just work all day – *with His help* – to smooth out some of those Flaws...See there? It wasn't as hard as you thought it was gonna be, was it!

Today is Saddle Saturday!

Today is SADDLE SATURDAY! If you climb in the Saddle, be ready to ride! One way to interpret that is spiritually. I love looking at things spiritually, anyway. It's my favorite way to look at life. Best way, when you think about it. When you get Saved, don't just be a "pew warmer," be an active Christian. Do! Be! Remember Shakespeare's soliloquy? "*To be or not to be, that is the question*." Such a great statement. Listen folks, to "be" a policeman, a beautician, a seamstress, a fireman, you have to "do," right? Well, why should it be any different for a Christian? Being and doing will make for a great ride on your journey in Life! So, get in that Saddle and ride for the Lord! Live your Christian life to the fullest! What a Trip! (Ride 'em, Cowboy!)

Today is Saved Sunday!

Today is SAVED SUNDAY! When you invite Jesus into your heart and life, that's called being "Reborn," or "Saved." Saved from what? Saved from going to Hell to live for eternity. Thanks to Adam and Eve disobeying God by eating the fruit of the Tree of Knowledge of Good and Evil (He'd told them not to do that) sin came into the world. Jesus then died for our sins so we could go to Heaven and live there for eternity with Him. Make sure you're saved...today! Do not put it off. Read John 3:16, it'll help you! *"For God so loved the world, that He gave His only begotten Son, that whosoever believeth in Him should not perish, but have eternal life."*

Week 13

Today is Masterpiece Monday!

Today is MASTERPIECE MONDAY! It's a Masterpiece first and foremost because God created it. After that, Monday really stands on its own as a great time to start over on "stuff." I start over on one thing or another every Monday ☺! Trying to get that masterpiece just right. We've rested on the weekend, so on Mondays we're fresh and ready to go. Therefore, with creative juices flowing, plans are made, new recipes cooked ☺, new relationships formed, etc. Masterpieces are created by *you*.

Today is Tempo Tuesday!

Today is TEMPO TUESDAY! "Rate of activity in general; rhythm." Does your emotional life have a regular tempo, or do you move at an erratic pace? Meaning, do you have a motor (reason/vision/focus) that keeps you going at an even pace on your daily moves? Or are your moves interrupted by depression, discouragement, etc.? If it's the latter, that can be fixed. God is the Great Tempo Fixer! Make an appointment with Him and "get 'er done!" Your life – at an even rhythm/Tempo, will have you tap-dancing!

Today is Wisdom Wednesday!

Today is WISDOM WEDNESDAY! Wisdom is learned from experience. From "Life-Lessons." I've had several of those. Wrote a song about Life. Wanta see it? Okay, thanks ☺. Verses: *"Life is a book...pages to turn, cover to cover...lessons to learn; The stories are told...line by line...Sometimes they're happy...sometimes blue, always unfolding...till life is through. From sunrise to sunset, one day at a time. Another chapter...one more page, Years keep passing...memories are made; Hopes and dreams come face to face with reality...Struggles and heartaches...write one more verse, Prayers at midnight...help heal the hurts. Our strength is renewed down on our knees. The story keeps changing...from cradle to grave, one day there's laughter...then tears stain a page. Thru it all holding to that unchanging hand...Finally the book...will come to an end, the cover is closed...God lays down the pen, Then He'll lead triumphantly to Gloryland!"* Chorus: *"There'll be a happy ending someday! And the ending will be the beginning of a new page! Eternal reunion, with friends and dear loved ones, just shouting and singing...A book never ending! Oh yes! There'll be a happy ending someday!"* HOPE these words may help someone. Since Life is like a book, just want to ask you; how will your next page read?

Today is Temper Thursday!

Today is TEMPER THURSDAY! "Heat of mind, readiness to anger." To Christians: We're living in End Times, so any anger of yours should be directed at the devil for holding your loved one's hostage, for bringing any bad situations into your life/home, and for the evil you see in the media every day. To non-Christians: IF you dared to believe God's Word, then any anger you have should be directed at yourself for waiting *this* long to realize God created you, loves you, and made a way for you to live in Heaven instead of Hell! To all: Let's put our Temper in the right place...!

Today is Fruitful or Fruitless Friday!

Will today be FRUITFUL or FRUITLESS FRIDAY for you??? What are you doing with your life? Have a work/mission/vision/focus? Draw a big tree on a poster board. Every time you see a piece of fruit appear in your life from your positive efforts, place a drawing/picture of a piece of fruit on your tree. Fill it up! You'll have fun doing this! Be Fruitful, not Fruitless!

Today is Serviceable Saturday!

Today is SERVICEABLE SATURDAY! (Helpful, useful, fit for use.) We love our modern lives, don't we! Buttons and clicks make things happen instantly. However, if – for whatever reason – we were whisked back into the 1700s, alongside the lives of our ancestors, we'd most likely be grateful for anything that was serviceable! A horse and buggy, wood stove, shoot a rabbit to eat, etc. Today, on Serviceable Saturday, let's send up a verrrry thankful heart to God for our push-buttons and clicks, and ask Him to help us *never* take them for granted! He could've created YOU, and me, in another century. Today, we have such a Serviceable life, especially in America! Thank. You. Lord.

Today is Soothe Sunday!

Today is SOOTHE SUNDAY! Soothe means to quiet, to calm, to comfort. There are times as adults we've had to be calm, unruffled and tranquil when we were called upon to quiet, calm and comfort a family member or a fellow Brother or Sister, and it's a good feeling to know we were helping. Obviously, many mothers recall nights of calming and soothing their children as they grew from infants to toddlers to rambunctious kids. And, just as parents calm and comfort their children, our own Heavenly Father – with the best comfort of all – is right there to Soothe and care for us right when we need it, night or day. Just ask...

Week 14

Today is Musical Monday!

Today is MUSICAL MONDAY! "What!?!?" you say. "I can't sing or play an instrument!" Hey, nobody said you had to be an accomplished musician or singer to be musical. I'm figuring you at least *like* music, though, so...be musical! Listen to the radio or CD as you drive to and from work. Let your fingers tap on the steering wheel and your left foot tap to the beat of the music. Sing along with the artist. Doesn't *matter* at all if you can't carry a tune ☺! Psalms 100:1 says, "*Make a joyful noise unto the Lord.*" YOU may not like your singing but I assure you, *HE* does! Let 'er rip!

Today is Turn Tuesday!

Today is **TURN TUESDAY!** It's *our* turn to Turn lives around, folks! Not just our own, but the lives of our loved ones and friends. Time to get serious about what's happening around us! We can't leave it to pastors and evangelists any more. Never were supposed to anyway, but for sure not now. Put this in your heart today...It's YOUR turn to be a Paul Revere. It's not the British coming this time. It's the devil! If you read the Bible then you'll have to agree! Turn folks in the right direction. Turning is part of our job!

Today is Where Wednesday!

Today is WHERE WEDNESDAY! Where are you? I'll tell you Where you are...You are in the Present. Being "present" right now...is actually the only place you can physically be. Can't go back in time, can't go forward. The present is it. So, take *this* moment to breathe deep and let some joy roll in! It's your moment! Enjoy the present. It's where opportunities are unlimited. Think about that! You can change your destiny. How? Only you and God – your Creator – know what's in your heart and mind; what plans need to be made...or changed; what good you can do for someone. What a difference you can make in the world surrounding you. There's bad to conquer and there's good to do. Get your mind working! This instant only...is *Where you are.*

Today is Thorough Thursday!

Today is THOROUGH THURSDAY! Being the oldest daughter in a family of ten children, guess who cleaned the house! Using a broom, I'd sweep the trash from the floors into a corner. I guess my mom cleaned it up from there. As an adult looking back, I realized that I had not been thorough in doing that job. I did learn from my father-in-law, though, that being thorough on any job – big or small – builds better character. Today I try to be thorough to a fault, in any given situation. Clear it up! Finish the job right. Pray thoroughly. Live thoroughly. You'll live with a better character (yourself ☺). Don't start anything that you don't finish Thoroughly, whether it's for you or someone else.

Today is Fresh Friday!

Today is FRESH FRIDAY! Fresh when it's the end of the week? Yes, and that's why it's fresh! Though you may be tired, just knowing the workweek's ending is refreshing. Here's the chorus to a song my husband wrote: *"God's grace is fresh every morning, sufficient in measure for all the day through, providing escape for each trial we face, grace forgives and renews, and touches creation with love and salvation, like a rose is touched by the dew..."* Fresh...ummm, Fresh Friday is...well, Fresh! Nothing like it!

Today is Soaring Saturday!

Today is SOARING SATURDAY! (To Soar is height attained.) Jets soar into the "wild blue yonder." Unseen angels soar through the Heavens and earth, and though we don't see them, we know they're there. (See Hebrews 13:2.) Birds soar majestically through the air, making us wish we could soar, too. Well, we *can* soar, even without wings! "How?" you say. By putting your heart in tune with Jesus, just saying His name – which connects instantly to Him – and knowing He's "right there" with you gives you a Special Joy that allows your very heart and soul to SOAR! You can soar like an eagle in ANY situation during your day when you fly with the Lord. HAVE A Soaring Saturday! It's yours if you want it...

Today is Solitude Sunday!

Today is SOLITUDE SUNDAY! Oh, how I love peace and Solitude! How about you? A lot of folks like the radio on almost all the time. To them that's peaceful. Their norm. Nothing wrong with that, but it's not me ☺. I like the silence. Either way, there's a reason for being silent – at least for a little while – and it's to embrace the warm presence of The Almighty. So today, why not go the extra mile to make sure everyone in your household is experiencing that very God-given peace and Solitude, "whaddaya" say! See y'all Monday! (Hey, that's tomorrow ☺.)

Week 15

Today is Moral Monday!

Today is MORAL MONDAY! No puzzle here. No hidden meanings. No reading between the lines. Just plain speaking. To be moral "relates to what is right and wrong in human behavior." We all *know* the story of young George Washington, how he cut down the cherry tree. When his dad approached him about it, he told the truth because he'd been taught good morals. And you know the rest of the story, too, how he became the first President of the United States because he was trustworthy. Men believed in him and his good morals. Now, the truth is, *you* know the difference between right and wrong. You do. Period. So, are you a Moral person or not? Which do your actions say you are? Hmmmmm?

Today is Toughest Tuesday!

Today is TOUGHEST TUESDAY! (Strong but flexible and not brittle.) Mostly it's men that are thought of as "tough." Women are not as physically strong as men; we are equally or more mentally tough, though. (Just ask us ☺!) However, there are times parents have to play a tough role; most of us have heard of "tough love" that either you – or someone you know – had to use on their children when they needed discipline. It's harder on the parent than the child; that's why it's called "tough love." Other situations bring out the "tough" in both women and men. Seeing action in War will bring it out. You have to be tough to survive. I'm in a war, myself. Are you a Christian? Then you're in the same war as me, what about that! It's the war where the devil knows he can't win – because he's already read the Bible – so he tries to take as many "down" to Hell with him as he can. He won't be taking me down, because I'm Tough! I survive by holding on to the Hand of Jesus! Are you Tough? *HOW* Tough? Will I see you in Heaven? Only the Toughest will go...

Today is Whosoever Wednesday!

Today is WHOSOEVER WEDNESDAY! This Blurb is about You, no matter who's reading this, because if you're alive, you're a "Whosoever." Whosoever wants to can be an upstanding citizen, can go to college, can work, can purchase a "fine" vehicle, a home, if you meet the qualifications for these opportunities. But here's a great one; you *automatically* qualify for God to write your name down in His Book of Life, did you know that? John 3:16 says, "*For God so loved the world that He gave His only begotten son, that whosoever* (that's you and me!) *believeth in Him should not perish, but have everlasting life.*" Isn't that incredible? Here's a chorus to a song I wrote called, "I'm A Whosoever." "*I'm a whosoever; whosoever will believe. God called out my name in John 3:16, whosoever, that's ME!*" I'm soooooo glad I qualify for everlasting Life in Heaven! Sure wouldn't want to spend eternity in Hell. Why don't you open the Bible and turn to that scripture and you'll hear Him calling out your name, too, if you haven't already. Just answer Him and invite Jesus into your Life. He'll say, "*Welcome*, 'Whosoever!'"

Today is Trader Thursday!

Today is **TRADER THURSDAY**! Got any burdens you're dragging around that are sooooooo heavy? I know somebody that'll trade with you for them! What? Somebody will take your troubles free of charge? Yep, and He'll trade priceless peace and joy in return for them! See the Trader today! His contact info is in the B-i-b-l-e.

Today is Fellowship Friday!

Today is FELLOWSHIP FRIDAY! Lots of references are made nowadays to the "front porch." That's because it's missed. The front porch was where folks fellowshipped. Had fun. Shared burdens as well as memories. Fell in love. Though we live in a very busy world today, we can *still* have that front porch. Like on Facebook and other media entities! Visit somebody's front porch today...Fellowship a little and it'll mean a lot!

Today is Super-excellent Saturday!

Today is SUPER-EXCELLENT SATURDAY! Maybe today is not the day that everything is going along super for *you*...*But,* maybe – in spite of your not feeling on top of the world – you can make someone else's day become super-excellent ☺! "How?" you say. Hey, don't depend on *me* to create ideas for you ☺! Get that thinker ticking on how to make SOMEBODY THAT NEEDS IT feel deserved. Time's a 'wastin'.

Today is Sabotage Sunday!

Today is SABOTAGE SUNDAY! (Obstruction action designed to hinder war effort.) Spiritual summary: Your life is automatically involved in a spiritual war, believe it or not. As a Christian, it's time to plan strategies to stop the devil from interfering in your life! Did you know you could sabotage him? Yes, you can! You can sabotage his moves by calling on the mighty name of Jesus, and His power will fight for you! Have you ever tried it? No? Well, don't just sit there...Get that head bowed and start praying to the Lord and ask Him to send that devil packing! Sabotage that rascal!

Week 16

Today is Me Monday!

Today is ME MONDAY! *"Me?"* you say...Yes, you. Sometimes we categorize ourselves by the clothes and shoes we wear, what style and model vehicle we drive (even what color), where we choose to live, the messages we put on social media, where we choose to eat when we go out, making sure we go to a fitness center, etc. We try to impress the world we operate around, and we want them to be sure to know "who" we are. Both our actions and appearance are saying, "Look at 'who' I am. This is me, and all of this makes me Extra Special." Now folks, none of the above is terrible, as long as we don't allow pride to rule our lives, because then it's a sin. So, I just want to remind you that the bottom line is: "Me" just needs to make sure that we know the One we want to impress is watching what's in our heart more than what clothes and shoes we have on, where we go to eat, work out, and in what vehicle. Life really is not about "Me." It's about *Him*. When you get that figured out, you won't worry so much about impressing others with "ME."

Today is Terrific Tuesday!

Today is TERRIFIC TUESDAY, and it's gonna be Terrific the whole day because I *choose* for it to be terrific. You see, the choice is mine. *Mine*. I can choose for each situation that takes place to be terrific or I can choose to let some situations be destructive. YOU get to choose how to live *your* day, too. What'll it be??? I choose Terrific! Woohoo & yeehaw!

Today is Weather Wednesday!

Today is WEATHER WEDNESDAY! One dictionary definition of Weather is "to bear up against." We've all heard the phrase "weather the storm." So today, just know that we can all weather whatever storms come our way because we have the Master of the Universe WILLING to help us weather them!!! Isn't that awesome??? I have seen billboards on the side of the highways here and there that say, "*Together, you and I can face whatever today brings...Love, God.*" That's what life is about. Weathering Life's storms with God.

Today is Total Thursday!

Today is TOTAL THURSDAY! Many people have said they are encouraged by what I sometimes post on media. So, let me encourage you farther by reassuring you how "totally" God loves you. It's proved over and over in His Word. His Word is for YOU – personally – so it's then a fact that He loves you *totally*. He wrote the Word for *you*! He created every part of you and loved doing it. Takes care of you daily. Air. Food. Mobility, etc. Gives you the ability to be happy...and see things or people all around you that make you totally happy. Things that make you *so* happy you just have to smile! Now...Give of yourself Totally to *Him* and see what happens!

Today is Fabulous Friday!

Today is FABULOUS FRIDAY! (Incredible, astonishing, exaggerated quality). Hey, you've made it a whole week! It's been five whole days of ultra-busy, throttle-to-the-wall work. But, did you accomplish something extra-special this week that had nothing to do with your secular job? If not, you still have a whole day to think of something nice to do for someone. Maybe buy lunch for a co-worker, or play ball with your son after work. (You're still young enough ☺.) Fridays are always fabulous, IF you make them so! EFFORT is the key word. Today's Fabulous...all day long!

Today is Surprising Saturday!

Today is SURPRISING SATURDAY! How many days have you planned out that have gone in the opposite direction? Probably more than you want to remember. The way to handle surprises is to learn how to deal with them quickly. I personally do that by immediately saying the name of Jesus, even whispering it. *Then* comes the choice of emotions: aggravation when you had to – surprisingly – have your vehicle towed, fear when you spot a snake crawling through your flower garden, hurt when a loved one says something uncalled for, and the hundreds of other surprises that can present themselves. So today? Let's commit to greet any and all surprises by...surprise, surprise; using my method; say the name of Jesus quickly. Know what that does? Brings calm to your every surprise. Try it next time Life is Surprising for you!

Today is Send Sunday!

Today is SEND SUNDAY! You can Send letters through the mail, email, text, Facebook, Messenger, etc., and it's good that we can do those things in today's world. But do you realize those types of communication can send tones? Yep, that's the truth. You have to be careful with your words if you're not there in person to temper them with the right tone. Words typed a particular way present their own tone. So, what kind of message did you send in your last text? Something to think about...because tones can hurt. Send a good tone. Sweet tone.

Week 17

Today is Motivation Monday!

Today is MOTIVATION MONDAY! Does the word "Motivate" scare you? (There can be several levels of motivation; depends on what you allow yourself to be motivated to do). Doesn't take much motivation to be a couch-potato, but takes a lot more to work towards being a leader of your county, state or nation. Hunger will motivate you to find something to eat. A need to see a loved one will motivate you to take a trip. What about just using that free will that God created in you by choosing to get motivated? Do something unexpected for someone else besides yourself...Good motivation=satisfaction/peace. Get motivated! This is your chance and it is Motivation Monday! (I see you on that couch; get UP! You....can....do....it. See there? You *did* it!)

Today is Tenacity Tuesday!

Today is TENACITY TUESDAY! (Tending to hold fast.) A friend of mine said her husband was a Pessimist but she's an Optimist. She said that she asked him once what did he love about her; he replied, "Your tenacity." Tenacity is just not giving up. Going forward with whatever endeavor you're involved in accomplishing. Which reminds me, have you read the Bible straight through? No? Confession time for me; several years ago I realized that although I had read many books of the Bible, different verses here and there, etc., I had never started at the beginning and read it straight through to the end. I made a commitment to myself and to the Lord to do that. And I did. It took Tenacity to get through a couple of Books in the Old Testament, but I did it! I read every "begat," etc. I was glad I did. Now when I go to Heaven, I can face God with a clear mind. I read His Word that He put together for me. For you. Yes, *you*.

Today is Witness Wednesday!

Today is WITNESS WEDNESDAY! When we use the word "Witness" we usually think of someone with their Bible in hand speaking to someone else, but actually you can witness just from having God's Word stored in your heart, being able to bring it forth when it's needed, maybe while exercising with a friend, hiking with a group, having lunch with a few folks, even at a carnival having fun! Witnessing is fun...if you make it fun, and you can. (The Holy Spirit will help you; just ask Him.)

Today is Twiddle Thursday!

Today is TWIDDLE THURSDAY! Nothing wrong with it occasionally. Need to Twiddle, actually. It takes away from the stress that goes along with life-in-the-fast-lane in today's world. Have you ever twiddled? (I know what you're doing, you're googling "Twiddle," to see what it even means ☺.)

Today is Folks Friday!

Today is FOLKS FRIDAY! You may be a "loner" and not like to be around people, as a rule. We've heard the saying, "*No man is an island, entire; every man is a part of the main.*" So, do you really think you can exist alone? For instance, where do you buy your groceries? You depend on the trucker to bring them to the supermarket, and the workers there to unload them and put them on the shelves. Truth is, you need them. Okay then. What if you were stranded on a deserted island? You might make it a good while with no one else around; no other voices, no music, no highway noise as you drive to work, plus other sounds. After a while, you might decide you'd like to be around people. Today...why don't we look closely at EVERYone we come in contact with, and thank the Lord there are folks around us. Folks to share with and folks to just enjoy. See how many individual Folks you can appreciate today...Question here: Do they appreciate you? You are "Folks" to them, too, you savvy???

Today is Sandbox Saturday!

Today is **SANDBOX SATURDAY!** Remember? As adults, we sometimes get too serious about ourselves. Go back – in your mind's eye/memories – to the sandbox. Life was simple. Still can be, though. Your choice. Might take a few tries to make it a habit to refresh those earlier moments in life that refresh the heart and bring joy to an overwhelmed mind. Let it happen. It helps. You'll see. (Hop back over into that Sandbox...)

Today is Stretch Sunday!

Today is STRETCH SUNDAY! (To reach out, extend.) Do you ever wish there were 36 hours in a day instead of 24? I do. I've even been silly-willy enough when I'm running late trying to get somewhere on time, to ask God to make the time stretch a little ☺. When I thought of this word, Stretch, what I really thought was: Get outta the box! Live! Such blessings await! Folks, I'm asking now, how far do you stretch? Let's talk about mercy, for an example. How far does your mercy go for your children who test your patience, whether they're two or twenty-two? Waaaay down, I figure. Then guess what: God's mercy for YOU must go a whole lot farther than that! *His* mercy must dip *way* on down. I'm counting on it, as a matter of a fact ☺! I imagine there are situations and incidents that you could relate to me about (1) how you had to stretttttttch your mercy a good way for a friend, a co-worker, relative, and even a stranger; and (2) how *you* needed the mercy of someone else. Hmmmm? So today, let's just STRETCH our good emotions/attitudes, get out of the box...and live! Experience the goodness of the Life God gave us!!! Hooray, I'm Stretching! Let me see you Stretch!

Week 18

Today is Majority Monday!

Today is MAJORITY MONDAY! What categories of Majorities are you known for? You're probably "one-of-the-majority" in one thing/group or another. Maybe it's for your choice of a selected political party? Of causing trouble? Of giving your opinion often, or even being a "know-it-all?" Or, maybe you're in the majority of those who choose to be more peaceable: the majority who are aware of others' needs, of being a good listener, of promoting goodwill instead of turmoil, of belonging to fun groups that like to play ball, bowl, go fishing, etc. Hopefully that's the majority you're associated with, because you don't want to live your life so that others place you in the majority of negativism, which can bring you unhappiness and problems. Daily life brings its own cares without your adding to them by inviting more. Make sure your life portrays you in the Godly and good-citizens majority because today is Majority Monday. You can have a smoother life...if you want it.

Today is Trash Tuesday!

Today is TRASH TUESDAY! (Junk, rubbish.) Any Trash in your life you need to send to the garbage dump? Trashy music? Trashy magazines? Do you think Jesus would have trashy things in His life? Duh. No, He wouldn't. We're supposed to follow His lead, so take a trip through your house and see what you can find to throw in the trash. Get your whole family involved. (Will you be surprising your garbage man with two cans of Trash instead of one ☺?)

Today is Warmhearted Wednesday!

Today is WARMHEARTED WEDNESDAY! (Marked by cordiality, generosity, sympathy.) Warmhearted people are usually the ones who smile at you coming down the aisle of the supermarket, and make you wish you'd smiled at them first ☺. They don't care if you smile back or not, they're just gonna be their Warmhearted selves and go on their Warmhearted way. Are you the "first smiler" or the responder?

Today is Twinge Thursday!

Today is TWINGE THURSDAY! (Like a Twinge of conscience.) Have you noticed those twinges? Maybe you saw someone you judged to be "less than" in *YOUR* book of "rules for humanity," then had a twinge in your conscience. Have you ever *counted* how many times a day you do that? Maybe you're at work, watching television, or even scrolling on Facebook and though you dislike those twinges, you just keep on judging. You'll find when you back off from unnecessary judging the Twinges will stop. Go ahead, start counting...

Today is Fantastic Friday!

Today is FANTASTIC FRIDAY! (Unbelievable, extremely great.) It didn't start out Fantastic. No, at first it seemed doomed to be a loser's day. But you'd had enough of dreary days, so you decided to make sure this day would live up to the word good. No, great. Noooooo, why not go for the gold. Fantastic. You'd make this a fantastic day! There, you made the decision. How to make it happen? Speak it. Yes, you remember that scripture about the power of the tongue (Proverbs 18:21). So, you say, "This day is gonna be Fantastic because I *said* it will be!" (And it was.)

Today is Sandwich Saturday!

Today is SANDWICH SATURDAY! (To make a place for, to enclose between two things of another character or quality.) Ever been a Sandwich? You're the one that two different friends or relatives confide in, both precious to you, and they both have different attitudes about something, wanting you to either fix the situation for them or be on their "side." Not a good sandwich. What about being in a meeting at your workplace where there's a debate over something and you're the meat between two pieces (attitudes) of bread. One attitude wants mayonnaise but one wants mustard, and they want you to decide which would taste better. Silly analogy, but still you get the gist of what it's like to be a Sandwich. We don't like those situations and try to stay out of them, don't we! Life is too short for disagreements! (By the way, would you choose mustard or mayo ☺?)

Today is Supreme Sunday!

Today is SUPREME SUNDAY! (Highest in quality; the ultimate sacrifice.) This word brings to my mind the supreme sacrifice that Jesus Christ gave for us all. Jesus was thinking of you and me – and all of mankind – when He walked up Calvary's Hill. What a long walk that must've been for Him, knowing what He still had to face, already beaten and wounded so terribly. Here are some words from the chorus of a song I wrote: "*The most important mile He ever walked in His life was to Calvary for me and for you; The most important mile I've ever walked in my life was the one to the altar from the pew.*" Folks, I hope *you've* walked that mile to meet with Jesus! If not, today is the day to do it! He loves you Supremely. Don't you feel it?!??!?

Week 19

Today is Mirth Monday!

Today is MIRTH MONDAY! (Gladness accompanied with laughter.) Are you in good health? If you're not, could you use more medicine? There's a Biblical scripture/medicine that will come to your aid. Truly. Really. It's Proverbs 17:22 and says, "*A merry heart doeth good like a medicine.*" And I'm here to tell you it works, as millions of people can verify. You'll be so glad you followed that scripture that, your mouth will curl in mirth even as you keep reading it! Life will begin to look better! Choose to read funny things periodically that make you laugh, and make sure that you laugh *good*! Just let that laughter roll out of you! Humor and laughter make a Mirth Monday! Go for it! (Ever see someone laugh so hard their belly jiggles?)

Today is Tact Tuesday!

Today is TACT TUESDAY! Are you a Tactful person? Considerate of others? Are you the first to "give way" in most physical movements? Two walking down a sidewalk for instance, and one needs to move over; is that you? Same with driving, are you the one that allows even the arrogant drivers to "have their way?" If you're that tactful person, you're to be commended. Don't let anyone tell you that you're too meek or weak or such. Just because you're tactful doesn't mean you don't take up for yourself when you need to. Look at Jesus: He was laid back, etc., but He got rightfully and righteously mad at the thieves in the Temple. It's all in the timing; the situations. Again, are you Tactful? Good, then move out of the passing lane so I can get by! That's me behind you, honkin' ☺

Today is Wonderful Wednesday!

Today is WONDERFUL WEDNESDAY! It is *not*! Not Wonderful at all. Too many bills, your sweet doggie has to go to the Vet, the A/C quit working in your car, you're late with the report you have to hand in to your boss, and the list grows longer every hour. You're "singing the blues." Hey, would it help you to know you're just one of millions who – right this minute – have as many or much the same problems as you? Yes, millions. Anyway, read this chorus to a song I wrote: *"There's always somebody else worse off than you, so lift the other brother up, he needs your prayers, too. No matter what the problem, praise the Lord anyhow, He's on the throne so we 'ain't got' no blues to sing about."* Today really is wonderful because you're alive and the Lord can take care of your problems! The key to a wonderful day is to help with other folks' problems, etc., and when you see how bad *theirs* are, that can make *yours* small in comparison. So great to know you don't have Mr. and Mrs. "So and So's" problems! Today IS Wonderful after all...!

Today is Tunnel Thursday!

Today is TUNNEL THURSDAY! (Passageway through or under an obstruction.) Are you traveling through a tunnel? I'm talking about a situation that you're trying to tunnel through, and you've determined to keep going forward till the end is in sight. You may be going through darkness throughout, but if you keep that light in sight that's at the end of the tunnel, you'll make it through! Jesus is Light. THE Light. Keep Him with you and His Light will show you the way through the darkness. Keep Tunneling!

Today is Finally Friday!

Today is FINALLY FRIDAY! In learning how to get victory and keep it, I experienced defeat. Then victory. Defeat. Defeat. Victory. Defeat. Victory. Victory. Victory. I had to go through some trials/valleys before I learned all of that, but I did it! Even so, each new trial will always present a challenge. Victory? Or defeat. Duh. Who wants to live in defeat!?! Not me! So, when I have a flat tire, instead of kicking the tire and whining with defeat, I just ask the Lord to give me His strength to get it changed, and He does! Victory! Finally learned! ("Finally" feels *so good*.)

Today is Stirring Saturday!

Today is STIRRING SATURDAY! (Active, inspiring.) What Stirs your heart? What inspires you to action? A particular style of music? A minister preaching a good sermon? A positive lecture by a famous Speaker? Your choice of a movie? Talking to a special friend? It's good for us to be stirred now and then. We need fresh inspiration, new actions, to keep our minds alert, to live life with a zest, so that we can then inspire others to do the same. So, go partake of your periodical stirring, then get your wooden spoon ready to stir someone else's pot. It makes the world go 'round nicely. Stirring Saturday. Inspires anticipation for what's waiting around the corner of Life...

Today is Surrender Sunday!

Today is SURRENDER SUNDAY! Napoleon had to Surrender. Who is Napoleon? If you Google him and read about him, you'll learn that he was one of the greatest military strategists in history. A famous saying is "Napoleon had his Waterloo." His defeat. He was captured in the town of Waterloo, Belgium and sent into exile. Just as Napoleon Bonaparte had to surrender, we do too, if we love Jesus like we say we do. What do we surrender? Besides our sins, we surrender *anything* that hinders us from doing what He wants us to do, what He plans for us to do...for Him. Remember the old hymn, "I Surrender All?" "*ALL to Jesus I surrender, all to Him I freely give. I will ever love and trust Him, in His presence DAILY LIVE.*" No, Napoleon didn't "freely" give in, but his life wasn't dedicated to the Lord. Yours is. Isn't it?

Week 20

Today is Magnetic Monday!

Today is MAGNETIC MONDAY! (Having to do with a Magnet.) I have been a magnet for every little situation to come my way that I didn't expect, and it took the time away that I'd planned for other things. Y'all ever had days like that? One thing about it, you won't find God complaining about being a magnet! He absolutely LOVES it when you give *Him* all kinds of needs to be met! Messes to clean up! The list goes on and on concerning what He'll do for His children! Magnetic God for our messes!

Today is Tour Tuesday!

Today is TOUR TUESDAY! Ever taken a Tour of the Bible? It's awesome! You'll see – in your mind's eye – a donkey that talked, a whale that swallowed a man then spit him out after three days, a sea that was parted so thousands and thousands of real live people could walk through it on dry land, a woman that was going to let a baby be cut in half, a man who spent the night in a lion's den and they didn't eat him alive, and the list goes on and on. All sorts of miracles and stories that you want to be sure you're knowledgeable about. Who knows when you might get into a conversation about the Bible and you'll be the ignorant one? Don't let that happen! Read it for yourself. You'll be wiser for it. You'll even find yourself chuckling now and then. Watch out, though; prepare yourself to fall in love before you finish reading it. Fall in love? Yep. With Jesus. You won't be able to help yourself. Take this Tour. You won't be sorry!

Today is Worthy Wednesday!

Today is WORTHY WEDNESDAY! (Deserving/having value/Jesus.) Sometimes we make mistakes that leave us feeling unworthy. Maybe it's just the tone of voice from your spouse or a friend, or maybe the devil reminded you of a long-ago choice that made you feel unworthy. He's good at that. However, it only takes remembering that you knelt before the Lord and asked Him into your heart to know who you really are; Royalty! A child of a King! Worthy! A brand-new person! You have value to the only one that matters: Jesus Christ. So, up with the chin! Hold your head up, Worthy Person!

Today is Trivia Thursday!

Today is TRIVIA THURSDAY! (Unimportant matters.) Trivia can be fun. Think outside the box. Look around you and pick subjects that would be fun to know more about. (Then...google, what else ☺!) In days gone by, to look up information you'd have to go to your bookshelf and search in your encyclopedias. What! You don't know what an encyclopedia is? Yikes, well...google THAT ☺! Trivia is fun! Get your thinking cap on. (A story in the Bible you've always heard about but never read?)

Today is Flattering Friday!

Today is FLATTERING FRIDAY! (To praise excessively from motives of self-interest.) Two points to make about this word. Words of flattery – when they're not sincere – can lead you into trouble. Be careful and learn to look at situations and pray, "Lord, help me to know if these words are from you or from the enemy." Remember the devil is not a guy in a red suit with a pitchfork. I wrote a chorus that says, "*Look behind the roses, look behind the roses, look behind the roses for the thorns...The devil does not come to us...in ugly form, so look behind the roses for the thorns.*" Roses (or something equally nice and pretty) sometimes keep us from seeing the thorns that hurt. Another use of flattery is when the words are sincere and *you* use them on someone else. You can *make another person's day* by thanking them for their smile, their new hairdo, etc. Flattery used well is a form of giving. What do you think Jesus would do? Give. So, go Flatter a friend.

Today is Storage Saturday!

Today is STORAGE SATURDAY! (Space available for Storing something.) I'd like to know what you have stacked in your Storage. You don't have a storage space? Of course, you do! Your brain is a Storage place for millions of thoughts, pictures, plans, memories, somewhat – actually – like a computer stores files. You delete some thoughts through the years, store others that are new. Every day when someone who works with computers opens theirs, different files are there to view. So what files are you opening in your storage today? Some files don't need to be worked on, but some do. Sometimes we all move thoughts to the back of our storage until we're better equipped and ready to deal with them. Others stay in the front. One file in your Storage you always need to keep near the front is a picture of Jesus. Sweet Jesus. Do you have a picture of Him in your home? You DON'T??? And why not, I say! He's the reason you're alive! The reason you have a Storage at all! Get a picture of Him, hang it in your home so you can memorize it, then it'll always be in your Storage! Have a great day, now, okay?

Today is See Sunday!

Today is SEE SUNDAY! Yes, See. Your eyes happen to be the best camera lens ever created. No matter the stunning pictures we are privileged to look at – and we've all seen some that touch our hearts and give us a glimpse of "being there" – seeing something in person just can't be beat. We also see with our mind's eye, imagining what was or what can be. Additionally, we can "see" a situation or scene spiritually, IF we are a Christian and have grown enough effectively in the Lord. When you "see" spiritually what's happening, then you know how to proceed, hopefully with Godly wisdom. I especially love to hear about folks who've had an NDE (Near-Death Experience). What a scene to See! One day, those who said "yes" to Jesus will see all of Heaven. All the loved ones who are already there are now "Seeing" everything. Will you be there? Will you?

Week 21

Today is Measure Monday!

Today is MEASURE MONDAY. (Estimate the value or effect quality of something.) How do you measure your days? Do you determine the worth of your day, your time and your life by someone else's standards or *their* likes and dislikes? Do you allow someone else's attitude to determine your outlook? More importantly, if their attitude is negative and influencing or governing yours, are you so inconsiderate as to pass that on to another person – one that possibly doesn't need to hear your negativism at that particular time? Hey! Take stock of yourself! Truth is, the ultimate measuring stick we should all use is the Word of God! It will surely change the measure of our own selves. Just try an inch a day. Before you know it, you'll advance a foot, then a yard, and first thing you know you'll be going an extra mile for someone, all because you Measured yourself! You can do it!

Today is Trample Tuesday!

Today is TRAMPLE TUESDAY! (To tread heavily.) It shows good character when you're careful to not Trample on the feelings of others with your inconsiderate speech or actions. The only Being you *ever* should trample is the devil. "There's really a devil?" you say. You can count on your sweet molasses and bottom dollar there is! He's real and he's out to make your life miserable. So, trample him today! How? Quote scripture. He *hates* that. Say the name of Jesus with sincerity and he'll run. You may have several chances to do this in twenty-four hours because of his persistence, but hey, today is Trample Tuesday! Stomp!!

Today is Wholesome Wednesday!

Today is WHOLESOME WEDNESDAY! (Sound in body, mind and morals.) Although there's always a fair percentage of immoral people in any country, America has been known for its good morals; folks like George Washington. George, only one person, influenced his wholesome living onto a small group, who passed it on to larger groups, bigger areas, then to a whole nation. So, keep living your wholesome moral life. No telling who or how many folks/areas you'll influence. You see, although George's influence lasted for hundreds of years, morals have gradually slipped out our nation's back door, and America now needs *YOUR* Wholesome influence!

Today is Trim Thursday!

Today is TRIM THURSDAY! (To free of excess by clipping or cutting.) We trim our lawns, we trim our trees, our rosebushes, our hair, nails, beard, mustache, etc. Physical and material things. What about seeing if our habits need trimming...Hmmm? Since today is Trim Thursday, I say, get your Trimmers out!

Today is Forethought Friday!

Today is FORETHOUGHT FRIDAY! (Thinking, planning out in advance.) God loves a plan. That's very evident because from the beginning, He's had the Master Plan. It's still His Plan today. It's never changed one iota. In me learning He loves a plan, and *I* love a plan, when it's time to record a new project (CD), I get excited. A WHOLE lot of forethought goes into it. Choose songs to write from my file of inspired subjects, write them, arrange them, go into the studio and record, choose the title for the CD, make the picture that'll go with the title, then voila! A new CD! All because of using forethought for a plan that we give to God, who helps us at every turn and blesses; because the plan we give Him is (This is important!) according to His Will. Do you put Forethought into your plans? Do you present those plans to your Heavenly Father? Your first Forethought...listen up here...is to include HIM in your plans!

Today is Sack Saturday!

Today is SACK SATURDAY! (To dismiss/tackle.) The word Sack is used a good deal in sports, i.e., "He sacked/tackled so and so good, didn't he!" What "he" did was "take care of" the opposition. Who's the opposition in *your* life? I hope you don't have any human enemies, but I'm sure you have the same enemy that I do, whether you're a Christian or not; it's the devil. *He's* the one you want to sack. God sacked him good when he threw him out of Heaven, didn't he! He now tries to get back at our Father by aggravating us/dragging us down, but you don't have to put up with that! There are enough scriptures in the Bible that'll tell you exactly how to get him sacked out of your day, so get busy and find those. Maybe write them down and place them around your house so you can see them and quote them regularly. The Word will never let you down! So, get busy Sacking!

Today is Salutary Sunday!

Today is SALUTARY SUNDAY! (Salutary is a statement of welcome or greeting.) Usually when you see your spouse after you wake up in the morning, you greet them with a "Morning", or "Hi", etc. Same thing when you arrive at work; "Morning, is the coffee ready ☺?" Before you know it, the whole day has passed and guess what...you haven't even said hello to the One that gives you the voice to speak in the first place; your Heavenly Father! Shame on you. He should be the first one you say "Good morning" to, before your feet even touch the floor. A loving Salutary! Start tomorrow morning doing it right!

Week 22

Today is Magnanimous Monday!

Today is MAGNANIMOUS MONDAY! (Showing nobility of feeling and generosity of mind.) What magnanimous feat can you make happen today? (Does that make you think of Superman or Superwoman?) You might need to be reminded that some of the deeds you could do for someone might seem small or insignificant in your eyes, but to them it's a large blessing, much appreciated, and God will surely smile on you for doing them! So, hop to it! Get your "Magnanimous mind" busy thinking of super feats you can perform! (Don't be trying to fly off a building, though ☺!)

Today is Toil Tuesday!

Today is TOIL TUESDAY! Do you Toil in the secular workplace? Or, do you toil as a homemaker? Either way, our population worries about making a living, providing food, shelter and clothing for our families. Gonna give you a scripture that talks about toiling. Luke 12:27 says, "*Consider the lilies how they grow: they toil not, neither do they spin. And yet I say unto you that Solomon in all his glory was not arrayed like one of these.*" What that says is that flowers grow beautifully, and they don't even work! Yet God takes care of them, so why would He not take care of His children! Verse 28 continues, "*If then God so clothe the grass, which is today in the field and tomorrow is cast into the oven, how much more will He clothe you, O ye of little faith?*" So, you see? God is promising to take care of us, day by day. Do not worry... JUST.HAVE.FAITH.IN.HIM. Toiling is our way of life, friend, but trust...you must.

Today is Whisper Wednesday!

Today is WHISPER WEDNESDAY! Why not be different today and do something out-of-the-norm...Whisper a prayer or a praise all the way to Heaven, and watch for God to let you know He heard you! A lonnnnnng distance? Nah. You see, God is omnipresent, that means He's all around you – *every*where – and can hear your faintest whisper. Don't just whisper once; see how many times you do it in one day, knowing He's listening right then! (You can even Whisper a secret to Him ☺☺☺.)

Today is Treaty Thursday!

Today is TREATY THURSDAY! (The act of negotiating.) Is there anybody you need to meet with, to settle something between you? Doing that will surely let you sleep better at night. Need to straighten some things out with the Lord? Only thing is He doesn't negotiate. His way or no way! But His way IS THE BEST! So, sign that Treaty with Him by saying, "Your will, your way, I obey." What *peace*...!

Today is Flourish Friday!

Today is FLOURISH FRIDAY! (Thrive, prosper, to grow luxuriantly.) To thrive or flourish at something important to you is a good thing. What do you thrive at? Being the best neighbor that you can be? Being nice to your sweet mother-in-law ☺? Doing your job well? Being a good parent? Using a special talent? Exercising well? Staying in touch with God? Hmmmmm? Not so good on that one? Let's get to work on it, okay? There's nothing like spiritual peace winning over worldly success. Flourish (grow) in His Word!

Today is Survey Saturday!

Today is SURVEY SATURDAY! (To examine, scrutinize.) We do that to others all the time, don't we...We criticize people, to ourselves, sometimes to others. We make judgment calls without knowing situations. Couldn't we make better use of our time? What's that scripture where Jesus talked to the men who were gonna stone the woman? Oh yes, I remember. John 8:7, *"He that is without sin among you, let him first cast a stone at her."* (Do you carry stones around in your pocket???)

Today is Spurring Sunday!

Today is SPURRING SUNDAY! (To urge, incite to action.) A popular belief in the Christian world is that our loved ones – who are already in Heaven – can cheer us on the journey we haven't finished yet. That comes from the scripture Hebrews 12:1. That's great, but no matter what, I always choose to spur myself forward in whatever endeavor I'm endeavoring ☺. It's good if we can take the initiative and go forward by ourselves. It's really easy, knowing what you know. (The encouraging Word of God.) I have a song called "*Knowing What I Know*." How can we lose/fail when we know The Word? I'm not saying that I haven't failed, I surely have. But I shouldn't. I've been known to make the statement, "Hey, no soldiers plan to knock on our door, coming to hang us like they did Jesus, so we can make it!" That alone should urge us to keep on keeping on, folks. We have every reason to be joyful, come what may! So, Spur-up your spirit and stay in the journey to Heaven! Giddyup!

Week 23

Today is Magnitude Monday!

Today is MAGNITUDE MONDAY! (The importance, caliber, quality of something; great size or extent.) Have you ever walked outside at night and just stood there and looked up at the zillions of stars blanketed by the background of darkness? The magnitude of what God spoke into existence is something only He can understand. Astrologers have studied the Heavens for centuries but still cannot come close to what's "out there." Only God knows, and He's not telling ☺. His Magnitude is limitless. He's God. The Great I Am. It's humbling to realize that the God of the Universe wants to walk and talk with little ol' me. And you. Have you had your walk with Him today?

Today is Twinkle Tuesday!

Today is TWINKLE TUESDAY! Precious is the person that has a Twinkle in their eye that inspires others to portray one. Because portraying one is not always easy in the face of sorrow, disappointment, and all the other "dis's" life brings. It can be done, though. We've probably all heard the commercial, "What's in *your* wallet?" Well, what's in *your* eyes? Hope it's a Twinkle. You never know who might need to see it...Think about that, okay?

Today is When Wednesday!

Today is WHEN WEDNESDAY! Your answer to a question is sometimes, "When I can get around to it." Well, *when*, then!?! Could "when" be right now? Today? "When" should actually be the present, because we're not guaranteed the next day, nor the next hour. So, what you need to do is plan "when" you're going to do whatever's on your "Honey-Do" List, since that's usually why the "when" question is asked ☺. Planning is good. Put structure to your free time and make things happen. Have fun "getting around to it." Getting around to what? *When*, that's what. When you finish that list, then you'll know *where* When went. (Are we laughing now ☺?)

Today is Tricky Thursday!

Today is TRICKY THURSDAY! (Giving a deceptive impression of easiness.) Like Life. It'll throw us a curve sometimes when we're obviously expecting the road to stay straight. Part of the "tricky" things in life is to learn from them. Grow. Wise up. Then when the tricky places come up again, you can show the Tricky things a Trick or two...Righto! (I'm getting a little dizzy just *looking* at these Tricky curves ☺.)

Today is Forceful Friday!

Today is FORCEFUL FRIDAY! (Effective, to compel, to press, to impose.) Don't tell me you're one of those who has to force themselves to get up in the mornings. You're not a morning person? Too bad, because you need to get up and at 'em pretty quick and get some force in your limbs; there are a lot of unknowns "out there" that are liable to come your way today unexpectedly, and you're gonna need to be forceful to get through it all. Truth is, the devil is the one who's at the center of "forcing" others to be pushy with you. So, whaddaya do? Be forceful to him! Let him know who your *Force* is! Jesus Christ! When forces become forceful during your day, use this scripture: James 4:7, *"Submit yourselves therefore to God. Resist the devil and he will flee from you."* See how easy it is to be Forceful?

Today is Sensational Saturday!

Today is SENSATIONAL SATURDAY! (Exceedingly great.) Why is it exceedingly great? Number one, because God has given you another day of life. Number two, because you have one more NEW opportunity of several waking hours to make this day the greatest it's ever been for someone else. Just think; this is the chance you've been waiting for to give a loved one a gift they're not expecting – an item they said they'd love to have, and they just mentioned it to you in a passing conversation. What a feeling that is, to make someone happy! When you're on the giving end, your heart and life will be exceedingly blessed, making your day – and your recipient's – a Sensational day!

Today is Shouting Sunday!

Today is SHOUTING SUNDAY! "I've never Shouted," you may say, meaning at church, thinking church is the only place to shout. Well, it's not. I've shouted many times through the years, at home by myself, when the joy of the Lord would just fill my cup (heart) to overflowing, when I'd be thinking about a particular blessing that He had given me. He's great at that. So, how can we not shout in joy and praise about those blessings? We can shout even while we're mowing the lawn, in the shower, or driving someplace. Shout for joy! Let me hear it ☺!

Week 24

Today is Maximum Monday!

Today is MAXIMUM MONDAY! (Greatest quantity obtained; period of highest development.) Did you get all you intended to get out of today? No? Why not? Oh, you were still feeling unfocused from relaxing over the weekend? Well, perhaps you could still say you did your maximum today, if you hadn't set your goal so high. Most of us usually set our expectations on what we *want* to see happen/accomplish but can't always reach that. No problem, just re-set your Maximums for each Monday a little lower. (See how easy that was?) Enjoy life. Quit being so hard on yourself.

Today is Tool Tuesday!

Today is TOOL TUESDAY! Wanta be a hammer? A screwdriver or a pair of pliers? If you're a Christian, God considers you a Tool. My husband was a tool that God used to bring about one of the most popular Gospel songs ever heard; "*God Walks the Dark Hills*." His group was slowly putting together their finances to record an album, and a co-worker said to him, "My sister has written a song you might like. She's pretty well-heeled financially and I think she would help you record your album if you'd put her song on it." It all came together as he'd said (The story in detail is on lewisandlewis.org/song stories) and the group titled their album "*God Walks the Dark Hills*." One night they were singing with the famous group, *The Happy Goodmans*, and passed the song along to them. The rest is history, and perhaps you're one that's been blessed by that song. All because my sweet husband was God's Tool...to bring that song to the masses. Now, want to be God's hammer? Screwdriver? Pliers? He'll use you and you'll be forever blessed!

Today is While Wednesday!

Today is WHILE WEDNESDAY! (A period of time.) "While" you're driving to run errands, you can use that "while" to plan part of a dream, you can thank God for umpteen blessings, catch up on memorizing scripture, sing a song. Then a little later, in another while, you'll accomplish something else, or even rest a while. Today in the many "whiles" you have, consider all the whiles in your lifetime you've already had. If you're reading this today, you've had a few million "whiles" to thank the Lord for, haven't you! Use today's "While" wisely.

Today is Treasurer Thursday!

Today is TREASURER THURSDAY! (A guardian of a collection of Treasures.) Men? You're the guardian/treasurer of your family and God looks to you to be just that. There should be nothing more precious to you than your family. It's your responsibility to make sure you introduce them to God, that your family goes to church, and that your children are raised in a Godly environment. Sadly, this doesn't happen nearly as much as it needs to. Are you one of the men who are afraid if they force their family go to church, that you won't be a favored parent? Don't you see? WHEN you stand up for the Lord, He's going to make everything work more smoothly for you. He will bless you for being a good Treasurer, and it's never too late to become a better one. All you have to say to your family is, "Today we're changing some things in our home." Then change them. You're the Treasurer. It's up to you. God has already given you the job. Now do it.

Today is Forthright Friday!

Today is FORTHRIGHT FRIDAY! (Going straight to the point.) Well, this might not describe ladies – as a whole, that is. Why? Because when we speak, we tend to go through every detail of a situation before we finally get to the point. Can't really say men get right to the point, either, can we? Because a lot of the time they speak in grunts ☺, monosyllables, etc. We ladies mostly have to drag communication out of our men. But may I say that I do TRY to get to the point in telling whatever I'm telling, I just want to be sure what I'm telling will be understood...every detail of it ☺. Let's have fun today! It's Forthright Friday, so all day long guys and gals – let's all see just how straight to the point we can be with everything we say, from the first "Hello" to the end of the day's "Bye." (Guys please cooperate, okay?) It'll be Forthright, alright ☺☺☺.

Today is Synthetic Saturday!

Today is SYNTHETIC SATURDAY (Produced artificially; fabricated for special situations to imitate realities.) Do you present yourself to some people one way, yet fabricate another personality for a different set of folks? Are you synthetic? Synthetic isn't "the real deal." That would be like the difference between a real fur coat and a faux (man-made) fur. Hadn't you rather be known as real? Don't you want to have a good opinion of your own character? Don't let yourself become artificial/synthetic. Synthetic character, yuck.

Today is Serene Sunday!

Today is SERENE SUNDAY! (Utter calm and unruffled repose/ease.) By and large, most of the world connects Sunday with church. The devil, who roams this world, "...*seeking whom he may devour*" (1 Peter 5:8), loves Sabbath mornings and tries to get families in a bad mood before they get to church. Tries to ruin their Serene day. Why not train yourself to be aware of his wiles – every Sabbath morning – and stay calm in the midst of the whirl of hurrying to church. Defeat that devil! Serene feels better than upheaval. You know that already. So, keep things serene. One thing is for certain, the devil won't be Serene, but YOU will!

Week 25

Today is Modest Monday!

Today is MODEST MONDAY! Word modest means not excessive; decent, virtuous. Many of us need to apply this word in different areas of our lives. Eating, our dress code, our speech, actions, etc. Since this is Modest Monday, let's see how many ways we can use this word to change some things that'll cause someone else to notice them! Hey, maybe we can even make some of our changes into habits that will become our new norm. Nothing wrong with being modest! Modest is good, and good changes can only be a plus+++!

Today is Take Tuesday!

Today is TAKE TUESDAY! (Carry.) You Take a lunch to work, your purse/billfold. When you go on a trip, you take a suitcase or a carryall with toiletries, extra clothes, etc. Take is a common word, but its meaning covers a lot of areas. It's a word of action. Dos and don'ts. Wills and won'ts! You can take your "stuff" many different places here on this earth, but you can't take any of it into eternity with you. A woman was heard to declare she was having her money put in her casket when she died, that she was gonna take it with her. She might've made that transaction take place, but even if so, I can guarantee you that money is now dust ☺. The only thing that gets out of this world is our soul. That's it. You don't have to believe me, but if you don't, only one of us can be right. Don't Take a chance! It's simple. Just make sure you let Jesus Take *you* to Heaven!

Today is Welcome Wednesday!

Today is WELCOME WEDNESDAY! Many homes have a mat on their front porch or landing that says, "Welcome." If you have one, does that mean God is welcome inside your home, too? I hope so. As for me, welcome into my heart, Lord Jesus! Welcome into my Life! Welcome into my home. Welcome to my mind, where I surely need you to help me through each day, with all the clutter that comes my way at my place of employment. When I wake up each morning, I love acknowledging the Lord before my feet even touch the floor! I start talking to Him right away, asking His favor over every aspect of what He already knows is going to happen. And whatever happens, it's soooooo comforting to know that He's *right there* by my side! Welcome, Lord, you'll *always* be welcome! So *thankful* for your presence!

Today is Trounce Thursday!

Today is TROUNCE THURSDAY! (To defeat decisively.) No! Not to Trounce a live person! God is Just and He'll take care of that. The one you want to trounce is the devil! He's the one that keeps nipping at your heels, aggravating you, trying to tempt you to eat that desert you know you don't need, to yell a bad word from road-rage in front of your kids, to buy that *awesome* vehicle ☺ you know you can't easily afford, and you can add to this list, I'm sure. The good thing is, the devil can't win, can't bring defeat into your life, UNLESS you let him. It's your decision. You can say, "No, devil not today! Not today, and not ever!" Hey, feels good to have victory over him – in the name of Jesus – doesn't it! That Jesus name...ummmm, works wonders. It'll Trounce the devil...you *KNOW* it!

Today is Fluffy Friday!

Today is FLUFFY FRIDAY! (Something inconsequential, lacking in intellectual content.) Sometimes we need a day "off," no serious decisions, etc. So today, just treat yourself. Read a book when you could be paying bills. Hike in the park when you should be mowing the lawn. Have lunch with a friend when you should be doing some laundry. Let your mind rest. Let fluff have its way! Embrace simplicity. Breathe deep. Watch the bumblebees around the flowers. Tomorrow's another day that'll be packed full of family/weekend stuff, but today...is Fluffy Friday!

Today is Swim Saturday!

Today is SWIM SATURDAY! I never learned how to swim physically, but I can tell you that I learned how to swim through a different kind of sea through the years! A sea of troubles! Used the backstroke some, front crawl some, paddled some, and swam furiously at times. Sometimes even though we do the best we can and we're living like we should, "Life" happens. Thing is, if you just keep looking up, even though you feel like you're going under the waves, God is right there in that sea of Life with you. He won't let you drown! But you need to hang on to Him!

Today is Soul Sunday!

Today is SOUL SUNDAY! God created every human with a Soul. Your soul is what determines where you're going after you die: Heaven or Hell. You *will* live forever in *one* of those two places, no chance of staying here on Earth. You're leaving. If you left here today – and you could, thanks to health failures and accidents of different kinds, etc., – where would you go? Do you know for sure? If not, make *certain* you go to the *best* place...and that's Heaven. Read John 3:16 and follow through...Today...is your day. It's Soul Sunday! *Your* Soul!

Week 26

Today is Merry Monday!

Today is MERRY MONDAY! It's *not even close* to Christmas Day and you surely may not be feeling Merry and in a festive mode, but why can't you put some merriness in each day of the year! Actually...you can! Even when it's July or August and you're fighting the heat and in a grumpy mood ☺, it will help your feelings by reminding yourself that *you have the option* to be merry...just like during Christmas season; So, remember...if you're having some of those days right now, just do what you'll be doing during the "Merry" days; sing "Jingle Bells!" (Let 'er ring ☺☺☺!)

Jingle Bells

Jingle Bells, Jingle Bells
Jingle all the way
Oh what fun it is to ride
In a one-horse open Sleigh
Jingle Bells, Jingle Bells
Jingle all the way
Oh what fun it is to ride
In a one-horse open Sleigh.

Today is Toss Tuesday!

Today is TOSS TUESDAY! (To make uneasy, to stir up.) Did you realize you can toss someone else's day by saying the wrong thing to them – or speaking with sarcasm – when it wasn't necessary? Now, you *know* how that feels, because you've been the receiver a time or two in *your* life, and it didn't make you feel like you meant much to the world, so don't do it to someone else! Toss the *other* direction...Toss encouraging words to folks! You'll see them "catch" with appreciation. Now...don't you feel better? Don't just do it once, practice it often. Start today...on Toss Tuesday.

Today is Windfall Wednesday!

Today is WINDFALL WEDNESDAY! Ohhhhh, how I love those Windfalls that come in the mailbox sometimes when I have no idea they're coming! Nowadays folks can even send a blessing to you through online entities, and when you start to check your email, there's one that says "You've been sent X amount of dollars." What a windfall...! God is always blessing us different ways, and so many of them we expect – food, clothing, etc. – for which we're evermore grateful. But when He blesses you from somewhere unexpected, you know even more how much He loves you. Hmmmmm, wonder if WE could give HIM a Windfall...Bless Him by making efforts we haven't made before? Yes! Go ahead, give Him a Windfall! (You know it won't be a surprise for Him, He already knows it's coming ☺, but that's okay, He's looking forward to it, anyway!)

Today is Trestle Thursday!

Today is TRESTLE THURSDAY! (A braced frame serving as a support.) We think of the word as a trestle for a train to cross over a road, river, etc., giving strong support. I imagine many of us have had to be a trestle of support for *someone* in our lifetime. I love the scripture, Jeremiah 32:27 that says, "*Behold, I am the LORD, the God of all flesh: is there anything too hard for me*?" What He's saying here is simply, don't ever doubt that He can do *ANY* thing that needs doing, because He spoke this whole Universe into existence! So, helping you help others is very easy for Him, plus He loves doing it for you. Next time you see a train trestle? Equate it to your emotional strength. With God's power and might giving you His own support, you can travel your journey of life in His strength. You can count on *His* Trestle to support *your* Trestle.

Today is Forbearance Friday!

Today is FORBEARANCE FRIDAY! (Refraining from the enforcement of something; patience; leniency.) Have you ever wanted to run away from a situation, but couldn't for different reasons; or wanted or say something "smart-alecky" to someone that really deserved it, but you persevered and did the right thing? Even managed a grin, perhaps? That's forbearance, my friend, and when you accomplish that, you've grown in maturity. Kudos to you! Reckon how many times today you'll need to call on that Forbearance...

Today is Skipper Saturday!

Today is SKIPPER SATURDAY! (Master of a ship.) Have you ever wanted to pilot a boat? Take on all that responsibility of getting your vessel to its destination without any mishaps? Sometimes storms come and a boat is sunk. In the "old" days, pirates were big on sinking ships. We all sail the oceans of Life, and we deal with a pirate today called Satan. Here's my take on him, through the verse of a song I wrote: "*I launched out of port on this voyage of Life, my sails catching the wind...Never suspecting the perils ahead...or how my journey would end. For Satan lay lurking in the cold dark waters to run my vessel aground...But a Sea-Walking Captain stepped into my boat and it was Satan, NOT ME that went down!*" Jesus is the best Skipper you could ever have on your boat!

Today is Swap Sunday!

Today is SWAP SUNDAY! (Exchanging one thing for another.) I truly traveled – in my mind's eye – to what I term "up Calvary's Hill" one morning at 3:00 several years ago. I trudged up that hill because I was carrying a heavy load. I reached the top, handed my burden to Jesus – who I knew would be waiting there – and He took it, *then* handed Victory to me in return! What a swap! I was so much lighter walking back down that hill because of that swap. Try it for yourself. You don't have to carry that load around. Jesus will swap with you; your burden for His victory. *You* surely can't beat that Swap! *I* couldn't.

Week 27

Today is Majesty Monday!

Today is MAJESTY MONDAY! (Greatness of quality or character, Royal bearing.) Good morning, your Majesty...What, my friend, you didn't know you're royalty? You certainly are! That is...IF you have become a child of God, you're royalty! Now: That means you have to *ACT* like you belong to the King of Kings. Just keep your eyes on Him and He will guide your steps, train you, and most of all, love you. He's Majestic! A different King from the earthly kings. Pull your shoulders back, lift your chin and put a sparkle in your eye! You're Royalty!

Today is Truth Tuesday!

Today is TRUTH TUESDAY! Although standing for Truth sometimes means standing alone, living with Truth in your life is very rewarding. It allows you to sleep well, whether you're getting a power nap or down for the night. There are several points to make about the word Truth, but it would take a whole book to elaborate about it. Truth is from God, and it hurts when the world rejects His Truth. For instance, if a friend/relative is not a Christian, sharing the truth with them might hurt when they are rude in response to you, but they'll really hurt in the end if we don't share it. Hey, if you choose not to speak to someone about God's Truth, let your life/actions speak for you. There's a song my creative husband wrote about that called, "*Actions speak louder than words*." Truth.

Today is Wrap Wednesday!

Today is WRAP WEDNESDAY! (Enfold, embrace, surround, to enclose as if with a protective covering.) I've met people through the years who have wrapped their hearts with a protective covering because they've been hurt by someone and have made the decision never to be hurt again. Even though that's understandable, it's not conducive to a healthy, happy life. Don't you want to be happy? At least when you open yourself to being hurt, you're living! God created us for His pleasure, hoping we would make the efforts to enjoy the life He's given us here on Earth, so don't waste His creation...meaning yourself! Unwrap that heart. Embrace life. Let God do the Wrapping, and my, what Wrapping He will do! He'll Wrap His arms around you and you'll feel His love surrounding you and you'll know what real living is all about!

Today is Trench Thursday!

Today is TRENCH THURSDAY! (A long cut in the ground or in wood.) An old saying from previous wars has been, "He's been in the trenches," meaning a soldier was fighting battles for his country. Today, when someone has gone through a battle, whether marital, financial, health concerns or other things, it's said, "He's been in the trenches." Good thing is, there's NO trench ever dug that kept God out. He goes in the trenches with us, AND brings us out of them. There are short trenches as well as long ones. Are you in a Trench today? Look close beside you. You're not alone...

Today is Freedom Friday!

Today is FREEDOM FRIDAY! There's freedom after a battle between nations, freedom experienced from getting out of prison. Different battles bring different freedoms. There's always a price to pay for freedom, whether it's bloodshed on a battlefield or time spent in a prison. Let's talk about freedom from prisons. There are different kinds of prisons, like prisons of addiction, or hurts in the heart that create bitterness, etc. But guess what! You *can walk right out of* those kinds of prisons and have freedom! Oh, what freedom! Jesus Christ is the one Who can walk you out and...you can *STAY* out, with Him walking by your side 24/7. He paid the price for our freedom, so there's no price for you to pay. Want freedom today? Give Jesus a call! It's Freedom Friday!

Today is Singing Saturday!

Today is SINGING SATURDAY! Your heart can sing, did you know that? Really, every person in the whole world can sing. Yes, you heard me. Every person in the world. Now, I'll agree that not every person in the world can qualify to be on stage at Carnegie Hall in New York, nor even at their local Community Center, but everyone can hum a tune, even if it's just to themselves with nobody else listening. Music is a "universal language." If two strangers met from two different nations, not knowing their respective languages, then one starts singing, most likely the other one is going to try to sing along, or at least start smiling. Again, music is a language of its own. God created music. He loves it, and it doesn't have to be perfectly in tune. Sing to Him. From your heart. That's what He loves most. It "speaks" to Him. So today, it being Singing Saturday, sing! Let God hear your heart. Know what? It'll bless Him. He blesses us all the time, so today let's bless *Him* by Singing! "*Amazing Grace...how sweet the sound...*"

Today is Surpass Sunday!

Today is SURPASS SUNDAY! (To become greater or stronger, exceed.) In many things, from riding a motorcycle to writing a poem. From being a better spouse or better friend than you've been, to doing a better job in the secular world. From eating a lot of the wrong foods that you know are bad for your future health to spending time looking for better meals. From not paying attention to what's happening in your nation to becoming a better-informed-and-involved citizen! Set your own goals, be committed to them, get as serious as you've ever been about any plan you've ever made, then...Surpass them!!! Make yourself proud...of yourself.

Week 28

Today is Mission Monday!

Today is MISSION MONDAY! (Assignment.) You don't have to be qualified as a Missionary to have a mission. You *automatically* have a mission – wherever you live – the moment you become a Christian. "How can that be?" you say. Read Matthew 28:18-20 or Mark 16:15 and that'll explain your instructions for a mission field. It's called "The Great Commission" and it's for every Christian. Spreading the Gospel of Jesus Christ is your mission, in the field (the world) that needs to be harvested (introducing sinners to Him). Just living your life Christ-like is a mission, too. So be aware today of who appears on your mission field, because this is Mission Monday and *YOU*...have a Mission!

Today is Teacher Tuesday!

Today is TEACHER TUESDAY! *You* be the Teacher today! What are you going to teach? "I've never taught," you say, so you can't do that? Well, let me just clue you in to a little tidbit here, okay? If you're an adult reading this, no matter how young or old, you're a teacher. Believe it. Every day of your adult life – no matter whom you've been with – if it's been with one person or a thousand, you've taught them something. By the way you talked, by the way you stood, ate, drove your vehicle, played a musical instrument, gave a Presentation, sang a song, brought donuts to your Sunday School class, made coffee at work and so on. You get the picture. Yes, you're a Teacher. Like it or not. What are you gonna Teach today, Teacher???

Today is Warehouse Wednesday!

Today is WAREHOUSE WEDNESDAY! (To deposit, store in a room.) One warehouse that I'm personally aware of is our hearts. We store scripture there. Our minds are awesome things, full of facts and scenes that can be "brought up" in a second. Many of us have learned scriptures in our childhood or teen years, deposited them in our hearts, then years later something triggered the mind and up pops one of those scriptures learned, word for word. They've been stored a long time but they're still miraculously there in your "Warehouse." Today, on Warehouse Wednesday, why not wander down the aisle of *your* Warehouse and see how many scriptures you can find!

Today is Thorn Thursday!

Today is THORN THURSDAY! I don't think you need a definition of the word Thorn. If you have a rose bush, you've probably received a stick now and then ☺. The piercing from the point of a thorn will bring an uncomfortable feeling, for sure. The point (no pun intended ☺) of this Blurb is to bring to mind what happened to Paul in the New Testament. In part of the 2 Corinthians 12:7 verse his words are, "*There was given to me a thorn in the flesh.*" Verse 8 continues, "*For this thing I besought the Lord thrice, that it might depart from me.*" Then in verse 9 the Lord replies to Paul with, "*And he said unto me, My grace is sufficient for thee: for my strength is made perfect in weakness.*" When we run into a thorn in the rose bushes, at least it's usually for a second, whereas it seems as if Paul's was there much longer. Whatever, you can be sure that if there's a "Thorn" in your life, it's bound to be uncomfortable, God does point out that it's not too much for us to bear; that in His Grace we can survive it. Why? Because His strength is greater – and is there for us – in our weakness! I'm soooooo thankful for it! A Thorn in our flesh? Ha! I don't like them – no matter what form – but they're *nothing* compared to God's strength!

Today is Fulfill Friday!

Today is FULFILL FRIDAY! When you were in high school and planned your future, did it turn out as you'd planned? Most laugh and say, "No." One reason is because the Creator of the Universe is the "Boss" in control of your life, and He already has a plan for your life that He wants you to follow. Sometimes His plan for you is different from yours. At times He'll send you in a different direction than you anticipated, molding you to fulfill His Perfect and Divine plan – which is always BEST for you. It's up to you to realize that. The best fulfillment you'll ever know – from being a Graduate to your old age – is to *allow* Jesus to guide your plans...every day. You *do* know Him, don't you? If not, today is Fulfill Friday! Let Him fill you!

Today is Safe Saturday!

Today is SAFE SATURDAY! If you belong to God, you're Safe in His arms no matter what happens. He never leaves nor forsakes us. Our world today is a mess, but whatever comes, we're safe. Doesn't mean we won't have some bad times, just means He'll bring us through any situation that arises, and we're eternally taken care of in an awesome Land just a border away from the earth. What a deal!

Today is Synonymous Sunday!

Today is SYNONYMOUS SUNDAY! (Alike in significance.) If you're a Christian, you're supposed to learn to be as much like Jesus Christ as you can. Christian means Christ-like. Synonymous with. You don't know how to do/be that? Start studying the New Testament of the Bible and you will learn all you need to know. Give of what you have, serve your fellow man, love the little children. Start this very day! Don't put it off! No excuses, now...You can be Mr., Mrs., Miss, Ms. Synonymous, always, not just today!

Week 29

Today is Mirror Monday!

Today is MIRROR MONDAY! Usually at some point after you get up every morning, you look in the mirror and examine your looks. Is your hair in place, makeup okay, neckline gonna hang straight? And men check (a little ☺) while they're brushing their teeth, shaving, etc. That mirror is a great creation, isn't it! It reflects who's looking back at you. But I want to ask you today, do you ever examine your heart??? Just wondering. That mirror in your bathroom or bedroom doesn't reflect what's in that heart of yours and how you conduct your attitude, your life. But...there's another Mirror that will reflect to you an accurate and precise accounting of what's going on in your heart – in a still, small voice. But you need to listen. Great Mirror, our God.

Today is Trait Tuesday!

Today is TRAIT TUESDAY! (A distinguishing quality/difference in quality; as of personal character; a personality trait.) Do you have a distinguishing trait? One that sets you apart from others? If so, do you recognize it as a plus...or a minus? How do you think others term it? Now, are you one of those who will answer, "I don't care what others think of me!" If so, well...your answer just told something about the quality of your person. A good trait would be you being kind to children, older folks, and those less fortunate than you, and very important, being considerate of how you talk to folks. If we were all alike, the world might be a boring place, but to be pleasing to the One who created you, why not make sure the traits of your personality are ones that others would want to exemplify. You can analyze your qualities today, since you have twenty-four hours of Trait Tuesday!

Today is Willing Wednesday!

Today is WILLING WEDNESDAY! (Giving permission to yourself.) What are you willing to do with the day you've been given? What if God asked you to become a Missionary and go to another country; would you be willing? What if He urged you to buy someone a car that really needs it, would you do it? He knows your finances, what you can or cannot do. To be a Willing Vessel for God, you really have to trust Him. *Think* about that, okay? While you're thinking about how much you trust Him, think about the fact that He's the one that parted the Red Sea for Moses. If you can't be Willing to trust that same God – an awesomely powerful and mighty God – to handle your life, who can you trust?!?!

Today is Treadmill Thursday!

Today is TREADMILL THURSDAY! Sometimes we get on the Treadmill of Life and turn the speed up to the fastest point. We don't take time to smell the roses. A fast-paced life could be a short one, full of stress. Won't you please slow down? You're the one in charge of your life. No, don't give me all of those lame excuses. If you were given a diagnosis of three months to live, you'd see those excuses didn't matter much after all, so...get off that Treadmill! Smell the roses!

Today is Famous Friday!

Today is FAMOUS FRIDAY! What is it Famous for…to you? Oh yes, I know, TGIF ☺. That's a widely known cliché. So, if I asked you what the end of the workweek, Friday, means to you, what would your answer be? Oh, fishing all day Saturday. Cool. Talking about Friday being today, do you acknowledge the One Who planned seven days in a week? Have you read the Book of Genesis at the beginning of the Bible? If you haven't, you should. It's very interesting. Tells how God created the whole universe in just six days. "But there are seven days in a week," you reply. Yes, you're right, but God rested on the seventh day. The universe, earth, the Bible, you, Fridays, fishing on Saturday, it's all about God. He's very Famous! Do you know Him? He knows *you.*

Today is Sapphire Saturday!

Today is SAPPHIRE SATURDAY! (A gem of quality.) A Sapphire is one of the most beautiful gems you'll ever see. Speaking of gems, sometimes a little one-liner blurb that someone writes or says is thought of by many as a little "gem." I'm proud to have passed on a couple of those to my children, as well as to a sweet nephew of mine, and he remembers them to this day. Loves to tell me how they helped him. Let me pass them on to you, too. You might use them in your life, or better yet, pass them on to your children. One is simply, "*Be kind to yourself.*" That just means there's enough "stuff" to deal with in *daily* life, without adding additional self-inflicted addictions, habits, etc., to it. So, be kind to yourself by making your life as smooth as you can. The other blurb I passed on is, "*Do something with Life, don't let Life do something with you.*" Some folks allow the "winds of life" to just blow them wherever it wishes, when all they have to do is stand against the wind! Make better decisions! That's it. Hope these little gems will help you and that you have a Sapphire of a day!

Today is Splendid Sunday!

Today is SPLENDID SUNDAY! One definition is "excellent." As for me, splendid waking up, breathing. Splendid breakfast. Splendid daylight. Splendid job. Splendid family. Splendid friends. Splendid technology. Splendid age to live in. Splendid home, walls to keep me dry, warm and cool. Splendid comforts. Splendid church family. Splendid God, created me. Splendid Jesus, Lord, Master and Savior. Splendid Holy Spirit. Splendid Bible. Splendid life because God loved us enough to provide all of the above. Splendid, I say!

Week 30

Today is Mighty Monday!

Today is MIGHTY MONDAY! I Might've already mentioned before in this book about how I love Mondays, but I can't help but be thankful every Monday morning that it's Monday again, so I thought I'd pass along my "Mighty Monday" feelings one more time! Not just thankful, but thrilled about it! To me, Mondays are the most exciting day of the week. "Why?" you ask in astonishment, and I answer, "Duh!" See, to me it's the beginning of anything you *want* to start, or something you want to start *over* again since you weren't as consistent with it when you started it *last* Monday. Remember that old saying, "*If at first you don't succeed, try, try again*?" Well, here's your chance! This is Mighty Monday and your resolve is stronger now, mightier than last Monday, so, "have at it!" (Ready, set, go! I do *so* love Mondays!)

Today is Taboo Tuesday!

Today is TABOO TUESDAY! (To prohibit, limitation, restraint.) How many times in your life have you heard someone say, "That's taboo!" I've heard it a lot. That means, don't *do* it. It's either not safe, not right morally, not good to digest, and we could list more things that are Taboo. Your mind/wisdom/common sense will tell you if something is not safe. For instance, you wouldn't crawl into a culvert just to see what it's like, because you might get wedged in there. That happened to me, yes, me, a girl, when I was about nine years old. (In age I was between two brothers and pretty much a tomboy.) Somehow in trying to sit up, my knee was against the "roof" and I was wedged for a bit. Scared me! Enough about that ☺. Your conscience will tell you if something is not right morally, IF you'll listen to it. And guess what…The Holy Spirit will tell you what's Taboo! Listen to Him! I'm verrrrry thankful He gives me a red light or a caution light on whatever is not good for me! Have you heard Him lately? Hey, all you've gotta do…is listen. (Shhhh, quit talking so you can hear…)

Today is Whetting Wednesday!

Today is WHETTING WEDNESDAY! (To sharpen, to make keen, excite the appetite, incite.) You may have an appetite for cars. Or shoes. Fishing rods and boats. Purses. A new home. A vacation by the sea. And of course, food. Car lovers see a particular one on the road and it whets their appetite for that model. A roadside sign with a hamburger on it whets your appetite for a juicy burger. Some men can't pass up a sporting goods store without checking out new fishing gear. What about stories in the Bible? Remember as a child you heard the story about "Jonah and the Whale?" Now you're grown and it's time to get your appetite whetted for the adult version. Read it! It'll Whet your appetite to read more of God's stories! They're pretty awesome...

Today is Tactics Thursday!

Today is TACTICS THURSDAY! (Strategy, method, system, scheme, to follow.) You think the success of a fast-food restaurant was easy? Just decided to do it and voila! It happened? No! There were tactics to put into place, and as the saying goes, "*Rome was not built in a day.*" Success takes time. God loves a system; a plan. He followed His own tactics in creating the world. So, whatever strategy you've lined out for today, include God first and foremost. He'll guide your steps better than you can. You haven't leaned on Him yet? Good grief, you're missing out on the main Tactic of Everyday Best Living!

Today is Functional Friday!

Today is FUNCTIONAL FRIDAY! (Performing a regular/usual act, operate.) Well, here we go. It's the day before your wonderfully planned weekend, and though in the world's eye you have a spring in your step, on the inside your mental capacity is dragging because you've had several days of tightrope to contend with already. However, you're known for being practical, stable, functional, and folks know they can count on you to be just that. So, remind yourself of "who you are" and pull up those big-boy or big-girl britches and hop to it. Let that fake spring in your step become real and let it spread to your face. Grin. Smile. You can do it. Hey, look at you! You're Functional ☺!

Today is Stunning Saturday!

Today is STUNNING SATURDAY! (Strikingly impressive in beauty or excellence.) Stunning because you knew the rain that was coming down was needed, and you knew it was God who provided it. Then the thunder and lightning began, filling the sky with a stunning show, if you will. Stunning, when you think about it. You had plans made for today that did not include rain, but God is in control of the weather; you're not. So, you had to change your plans, no big deal. Instead of mowing the lawn and trimming the bushes (You were dreading that, anyway), now you can play Chess with your son. He's been beating you lately so today you'll show him that his "old man" has still "got it." Yay! What a simply Stunning Saturday this turned out to be!!!

Today is Separate Sunday!

Today is SEPARATE SUNDAY! (To disconnect; set apart from others.) Can you separate the good from the bad? Surround yourself with good friends/things? Leave the bad alone? Most of all, can you separate the Good Book from the bad reading material you've been choosing? Choose the Good Master, not the bad one? Okay, okay, you say you want names? Choose Jesus and the Bible, not Satan and his trashy stuff. There, that's plain English!

Week 31

Today is Magniloquence Monday!

Today is MAGNILOQUENCE MONDAY! What on earth does this word mean? Here are some definitions: "Characterized by a high-flown, often bombastic, pompous, overblown style or manner; use of grand or wordy speech to say something simple." I personally claim my simplicity. I'm lost when someone speaks "over my head" (No pun intended, I know I'm kinda short ☺), and since that has happened too many times to me, I thought I'd address it here today. If I can't understand what you're talking about, then there's no need for me to hear it. Save your breath and my time. If you know one of those people who likes to show their magniloquence when they're talking to you, the next time that happens just tell them, "You're Magniloquence is mind-boggling; check out Philippians 2:7 and 1 Peter 5:5." *YOU'RE* not one of those people, are you? I hope not, because if you are, you're just showing how smart you're not...

Today is Thrilling Tuesday!

Today is THRILLING TUESDAY! Have you ever ridden on a roller coaster? The flips and dips will take your breath, but they'll give you a certain thrill as well. I think we can liken Life as an analogy for that, don't you? While you're on that roller coaster you may think you're gonna fly off into space, but you don't. Same for Life. God keeps us anchored to His Love, and isn't that the most Thrilling emotion you've ever had?!? Roller Coaster Thrills on the way to Heaven! Life as a Christian is never boring, and I'm so Thrilled about that! Whoohoo!

Today is Wall Wednesday!

Today is WALL WEDNESDAY! Are there Walls between you and someone? Maybe you had harsh words some time ago and though you're still speaking, there's a "wall" there, which prevents the peace you once felt. Part of Ephesians 4:26 says, "*Let not the sun go down upon your wrath.*" Those walls for you might not include wrath, but you get the message. Today is the day to knock those walls down. Clear the air. How*EVER*....Pray first! *By all means*, don't do it alone! Let the Holy Spirit guide you. That way it'll work out smoothly, and that Wall will come tumbling down! Praise the Good Lord for no Walls!

Today is Talent Thursday!

Today is TALENT THURSDAY! (A particular gift or endowment.) Okay, to start this daily Blurb, what's your talent? Oh, you're one of those that say, "I don't have a talent." Oh, yes you do. Our Heavenly Father didn't leave you out. He has given a talent to everyone He created, so that means you, too. Pretty much when the word Talent is used, folks immediately think of music, but you don't have to be musical to have a talent. Talent(s) are variable. You see, you may have a talent for what's known as a "gift of gab," so you can call folks and invite them to church. You may sew well, knit or crochet, and can make needed items for orphans. If you are a great mechanic, you could keep a watch on widows' and widowers' vehicles. Oh, so many talents to use! So, figure out your Talent(s) and have absolute fun beginning a brand-new adventure!

Today is Forgiveness Friday!

Today is FORGIVENESS FRIDAY! "No! I don't *want* to forgive them. They do not deserve it! They made my life miserable! I shed many tears because of them! They were condescending and arrogant!" Those were my words many years ago. But I knew – that I knew – bottom line I had to forgive them because the Bible says I must or I will not be forgiven of my own wrongs. So, I finally forgave them, but you want to know how I did it? It was when I realized though I despised these people, God loved them. So, that put a different spin on *every*thing. Maybe there's someone in your life that you need to forgive, and maybe my little situation will help you, because after all, not only today, EVERY day is Forgiveness day!

Today is Sparkle Saturday!

Today is SPARKLE SATURDAY! Is your life filled with a routine? Does it need brightening? I know *just* the answer that can change your dullest gray day to one that Sparkles! The jobs that you perform day after day will no longer be routine. "What!?!" you want to know. Well, one answer is to learn one new scripture per day – or per week, whichever you decide for yourself – by quoting it out loud. Pretty soon you won't be just learning it, it'll be ministering to you, opening up your heart to receive it and count on it! Another answer is music. If you can listen to it as you work – either with or without headphones – be sure to choose uplifting music. Instrumentals without words are good for accompanying work. That way, words in a song are not distracting you from your work. *My* first choice would be Big Band or Jazz. Best answer to bring a Sparkle to your life? Ha! You know what I'm gonna say already! God knows exACTly what will put a Sparkle in your life – better than I can guess for you – because He *knows* you and of course, I *don't*. Ask Him for a Sparkle! He'll even change your Sparkle to a Shine ☺.

Today is Sword Sunday!

Today is SWORD SUNDAY! A sword needs no definition; it's been around for thousands of years to use in battles. The best one is right in front of you. Yes, it is! It's in your mind and heart and you can pull it up/out anytime you need it! Here it is. Hebrews 4:12, *"For the word of God is quick, and powerful, and sharper than any two-edged sword, piercing even to the dividing asunder of soul and spirit, and of the joints and marrow, and is a discerner of the thoughts and intents of the heart."* Learn how to use this Sword! It's verrrrry effective...

Week 32

Today is Marshal Monday!

Today is MARSHAL MONDAY! (To bring together and order in an effective way.) Probably when we think of this word, James Arness in "Gunsmoke" comes to mind. Or maybe we think of this current age when it has seemed as if rioters in our country have needed marshaling. Since a definition is "order in an effective way," what about your children? Do you raise them with enough discipline that you can take them to a restaurant or even a supermarket without eye-rolls from other diners/shoppers? Or are you one of those parents that allows their young to "call the shots?" You *could* turn things around so that *you're* the parent and the child is just that; a child. Children do not know what's best for them. A good Marshal simply watches over his people and disciplines when he needs to. That's all. So, "Hello, Marshal."

Today is Task Tuesday!

Today is TASK TUESDAY! (Ability to deal without giving offence.) Have a task today and you're not looking forward to it? Have another one you can't wait to delve into because you love doing it? Well, you're always gonna have both of those kinds of tasks to take care of through your life, from settling a problem with your teenager because they're pushing the rules, to weeding your flower garden. The fun tasks are easy. But how do you make the hard ones easier? Hey, that's easy ☺. Simple. Ask the Holy Spirit to (1) handle the hard task for you so you won't even have to deal with it, or (2) ask Him to give you the right words to say in order to take care of it smoothly. He'll do it! He's the Master Taskmaster! You knew that, you just needed reminding...

Today is What Wednesday!

Today Is WHAT WEDNESDAY! This word has so many definitions it was hard to choose one. So, I'm just going to address this subject: What about the Unfortunates of the world, the handicapped, etc.? Do you pass them by, not look them in the eye, as if they are a lower station person than you? If so, I wonder how that makes them feel. But for the Grace of God, that could be me or you. Haven't *you* ever felt unnecessary when someone you care about ignores you or treats you as if you don't matter? Read this verse about Jesus: *"He sits majestically upon His throne, listening to the saints rejoice and angels sing...But on Earth the scene is different, seems people all around us have forgotten Jesus' name. The King of all Creation, the Hope of our Salvation, though the world can't see. He just wants to be a part of His Family. Though rejected He still calls patiently, 'What about me?'"* What *about* Him, Reader? Have you ignored Him? Let me clue you into something here: Jesus, the King of Kings, the Name above all Names, is the answer to all the "What's" in your Life. Pay attention to Him! You matter to Him, now make *Him* matter to *you*!

Today is Truce Thursday!

Today is TRUCE THURSDAY! (A suspension from a disagreeable state or action.) Ready to call a Truce? Aren't you tired of the feeling you've been carrying around, seems like for*ever*? Goodness, what happened was eons ago and you're still wearing the cloak of hurt. And guilt because you let it happen. Your fault. You're gonna have to let go, you know. You don't want to mess up the rest of your life "toting" this around. See, I know the Truce we're talking about making here is with your*SELF*! Your mind and heart fight constantly about it. You've blamed yourself far too long and it's time to call a Truce. Know what? It's okay to talk from your mind to your heart. Tell yourself to turn this over to the Lord and walk away from it. You tried to be perfect and it didn't work. No one is perfect but Jesus. You, my friend, just need to live your life as perfect as you can, and when the imperfections show up, give. them. to. Jesus. *He'll* take them. Go ahead. He'll wait for you.

Today is Flat Friday!

Today is FLAT FRIDAY! (Lacking in animation, zest, vigor; dull, stale.) Have you ever pretended? I'm not talking about when you were a child and had an imaginary friend. I'm talking about after you became an adult. Let's "play" for a minute. Let's pretend that George Washington has "come back" and you are the one that's getting to present a modern-day United States to him. He's in the vehicle with you and he's astounded that we don't have to use horses as the only means of transportation anymore. Everything is beyond his imagination! Now, let's change the scene. George is gone. Jesus Christ is riding in his place. What scenes does he see while riding with you? Food for thought here. See, my Friend, you may not see Him, but He's riding in your vehicle already! When you realize that and address it, the day won't be Flat anymore. It's not Pretend, it's real! Jesus Christ rides in your vehicle! He's there when you open the door! This is NOT a Flat world, nor a Flat Life! It's thrilling! Whoohoo and yeehaw! Jesus is welcome in my car all the time!

Today is Superb Saturday!

Today is SUPERB SATURDAY! Superb means rich, sumptuous, supremely good. The word sumptuous means luxurious, splendid. Today as I write this it's raining in my area, PTL! Sure needed it! That's rich! Supremely good! I'm rich this Saturday because I know the God of the universe! He gave me this very day...to do what I will with it. Are you reading this? If so, then obviously He gave you this day, too. Make it a Superb day for yourself! Include God in it, and it will be even a more Superb Saturday! Even rain can be Superb! (As long as you have an umbrella ☺.)

Today is Swerve Sunday!

Today is SWERVE SUNDAY! (To turn aside abruptly from a straight line.) Today...concentrate on Swerving around those situations – that you already know from experience – are gonna upset you, anger you, cause you to say or do things that get you in trouble with the Lord. When you learn to swerve *rather than get hit*, you're learning spiritual maturity. You're "growing in the Lord." Makes the Lord happy...for *YOU*.

Week 33

Today is Messenger Monday!

Today is MESSENGER MONDAY! "One who bears a Message." Actually, everybody bears a message of some kind...on their face. A message of cheer, a scowl of discontent, even a blank stare that portrays an empty soul. There's a look in the eye that can send a message of love...or dislike. Expressions matter, friends. They matter. I love the pictures of Jesus because in His eyes you'll always see the message of Hope. What message are *you* carrying, Messenger?

Today is Transmit Tuesday!

Today is TRANSMIT TUESDAY! (To convey from one person or place to another.) Are you good at talking from your heart? If you are unable to communicate your real feelings, how is anyone else going to know how to react to you? Get to know the real you? It's said that communication is the key to a good marriage. Problems can be solved in the workplace – and especially at home – if feelings are transmitted through words. Be careful, though. Don't transmit with the intent to hurt. Transmit to make lives better. You can even start by letting your heart talk…with your actions. Box of chocolates? Yum! (And a small card that says, "Just because I can.")

Today is Why Wednesday!

Today is WHY WEDNESDAY! Why troubles? Well, here it is all laid out for you. There are two powers in the world, God and the devil. The devil only has power because God allows it. Why? To give you what my book is all about: Choices. To choose good instead of bad. You see, God gave every man "free will." He wanted us to have freedom to choose, hoping we'll choose Jesus over the devil. Heaven over Hell. Why? Because God loves us and wants us to live with Him in Heaven, and those that choose Jesus will live there for*EVER, w*here everything is PERFECT! In the meantime, the devil will give you all the troubles he can, plus try to keep you from choosing Jesus as your Savior. Why? Because he knows he's destined for Hell so he wants to take you with him before you accept Jesus into your heart. That's WHY it's vital that you choose Jesus *today*! Why? Because the Bible says we aren't promised tomorrow. If you have any more Why's, *WHY NOT* go to the New Testament and read God's whole Plan for yourself! Then you'll understand more about it. Don't procrastinate, just *do* it! (Don't you DARE ask Why ☺☺☺☺☺!)

Today is Trend Thursday!

Today is TREND THURSDAY! (A general movement, current style or preference.) You think it's others "out in the world somewhere" that are the only ones to initiate a trend? Not so, and I'll tell you why. You're smart enough to realize it, you just haven't had anyone to point it out to you yet. Well, I'll do that for you ☺. You live in *such* a great age in Time to be able to pull this off. Start a Trend, I mean. How? Obvious, if you please. Internet. Social Media. The world is at your fingertips through your computer. So, whether it's a different style of clothing, a musical endeavor of some sort, an abbreviation of words, etc., you can make it happen. Just look at how fast the green and purple hair trend became the rage; it was because pictures were shared across the world through text and online social media. So, what Trend do you want to start today? You'll want to make sure it's a positive one that God approves. Get His input! You can even just start one local, in your office, your club, etc. Go for it! You can be a Trend-Setter!

Today is Firm Friday!

Today is FIRM FRIDAY! (Solidly fixed in place. Steady. Not easily moved.) Is this you? You could probably add "stubborn" to the definition of this word ☺. When you firmly believe in something, you should not be influenced by outside opinions/beliefs. Speaking for myself, though I've had some bad days in my life, still my worst day has been Good, and I remain steady in that belief. *Any*body can live Life with a Zest, if they make that choice and stand firm on it. One thing I stand firm on is the Word of God. I'm unmovable on that! My feet are Firmly planted on it!

Today is Signboard Saturday!

Today is SIGNBOARD SATURDAY! Once I had a lady say to me, "I just know you're a Christian, I can tell by your countenance." (That's my signboard, you see.) I had just said a few words of hello to her, but still she could see my sign read "Christian." What a compliment! What does *your* Signboard say? Is it time to repaint your sign?

Today is Somehow Sunday!

Today is SOMEHOW SUNDAY! (One way or another not known or designated; by some means.) Well, I can see what the dictionary says about this word, and though many say, "I'll get it done *some*how," I can tell you right now that I personally KNOW the "how" part of the word. Not only that, I know the "some," part, too. When I hear choirs sing, "I'm going to Heaven somehow," I think, *Somehow*? *I'll* tell you about somehow! By the Grace of God, *that's* how! Listen to me, the "Some" is our God and the "How" is through His Son, Jesus Christ! Anytime you use the word "Somehow" in the future, let me just say here that it doesn't even really need to be used. Nope. Not at all. What you *do* need to learn to say is simply, "I'll get it done with the help of Jesus." Folks, He's our SOMEHOW!

Week 34

Today is Management Monday!

Today is MANAGEMENT MONDAY! (Act of Managing; executive skill; use of means to accomplish an end.) I'm a great Manager. I know I am because my siblings have told me that I was – over and over through the years – but I think they were being extra nice by not using the word "Bossy ☺!" It came natural though. When you have several younger siblings, you just tend to "manage" them, especially when your parents name you as the Designated Baby sitter. It was easy for me because I loved my siblings to the max, and to this very day that bond is so precious. The truth is, my childhood held good training for me, because I did go into Management for several years and was a pretty cool "Boss," or so I was told by my employees. One great thing I have learned through life, though, is to leave the managing of my own Life to the Master Manager, Jesus! He's the Very Best when it comes to Management! If you love Him, you'll agree...

Today is Transition Tuesday!

Today is TRANSITION TUESDAY! Sometimes a big change in your way of life can take more than one step. The Transition from addiction to freedom is a good example. There are all sorts of addictions – drugs, alcohol, smoking, caffeine, cell phones, electronic devices, etc. But that's not all. If you can't find time for the Lord in your life because it's too full of extracurricular activities, then you might be addicted to that. If you're addicted to something and want freedom from it, God can transition you from ANY addiction, that's something you can count on. You have to trust Him, though! Totally give it to Him, and trust. On a lighter note, before my first child was born, I was addicted to Dr. Pepper and crushed ice. Couldn't get enough of both. As soon as my baby was born, I wanted neither one, not even once! What a Transition - Ha! Painful, but worth it ☺☺☺ !!!

Today is Waterloo Wednesday!

Today is WATERLOO WEDNESDAY! I've already made reference to General Napoleon Bonaparte once in this book, but here's what to remember about his Waterloo (The town in Belgium where he was defeated.) Don't have one! Through the ages there has been a statement made by tens of thousands, *"If you do that, it'll be your Waterloo."* His defeat is why that statement started. He gave up. Surrendered to his enemy. That was back in 1815, but I'm telling you that today there's an evil enemy that's trying to take over the whole world, and it's the devil. His name is Satan. He's out to "steal (your children's minds/good habits), kill (your joy plus anything else he can) and destroy (your life.)" This is not what Laura Livingston Lewis made up to tell you; it's what God's Word tells us all. So, take it seriously. Don't. Allow. Satan. To. Give. You. Defeat! In the name of Jesus! Just say, "Today is Waterloo Wednesday for Satan, *not me!"* (Not today, Satan, not ever!)

Today is Tug Thursday!

Today is TUG THURSDAY! When we hear that a good friend has passed from this life, especially a young parent with children, it Tugs on our heartstrings for the family left behind, especially if the spouse left behind has a tendency to be bitter about it. It makes us want to tug them gently towards a more peaceful attitude, reminding them that (1) we all have an appointed time to die, and (2) most importantly, trusting in God at this time of sorrow and grief is crucial. He knows what He's doing plus He knows how each person is hurting. Often adults have to put their feelings on hold for a while and tug the children closer. They turn to the parent in trust; it's natural. Likewise, we need to turn to *God* in trust. He will comfort greatly through our sorrow. If we'll find a quiet place and tell Him how we feel, when we finish, we'll feel...a Tug, drawing us close to Him. And, that's where we need to be.

Today is Forge Friday!

Today is FORGE FRIDAY! (To move forward steadily.) When my husband, Ray Lewis, was the ripe old age of thirteen, his pastor asked him to be the speaker for the Youth Service one Sunday night. He said he studied all week long and had around a thirty-minute delivery ready. (He was just a very young Christian, not a preacher.) When Sunday night came, he was nervous, and after standing behind the pulpit for the very first time, he said that his whole speech lasted maybe three minutes ☺ But...he forged ahead. He didn't let that stop him. He studied God's Word and, years later, became pastor of a church, where his sermons lasted sometimes an hour! (Just ask some members of his congregation ☺) Do you have something you need to Forge ahead on so you can get better with it? Marriage? Raising children the right way? Learn Archery better, even if it's hard at first? Learn more keys on the guitar? Grow in the Lord? Forge ahead, Friend! You'll be proud you did!

Today is Scheme Saturday!

Today is SCHEME SATURDAY! (A systematic plan for attaining some particular object or putting a particular idea into effect.) I was driving along talking to myself one day (Do y'all do ever do that ☺?) concerning a decision someone else had made – which affected me somewhat but wouldn't ruin my life by any means – and suddenly realizing this, I said out loud, "It won't matter in the grand scheme of things." Having decided that, I felt better, because it put "stuff" into proper perspective. You see, the *only* thing that'll EVER matter in your life – in the grand scheme of things – is your destination when it's time for you to leave this earth. Do you understand that??? Now, in the meantime, I'd like to point out a couple of reminders to you that might seem to matter: (1) Name Brands are not what matters for the teens you're raising, but morals, attitudes and beliefs are! (2) Having the newest vehicle or the grandest home won't matter when you're drawing your last breath...in the grand scheme of things. The Grand Scheme of things can be described with very few words: Arriving in Heaven.

Today is Sweetheart Sunday!

Today is SWEETHEART SUNDAY! Do something for your Sweetheart today, just because you can. Your sweetheart may be your spouse, your child, your mom, or a sweet niece or nephew. Roses (or candy, cards and cute little trinkets/toys) should be given while you can give them! Hurry to the store now and pick out something! Tomorrow isn't promised...for you OR your Sweetheart...

Week 35

Today is Meditative Monday!

Today is MEDITATIVE MONDAY! (Intend, ponder, purpose.) What to do? Which direction to go? Have to think about it. Nothing wrong with a Meditative mind. Pondering is good. Don't want to end up making the wrong decision and heading the wrong way. There are lots of twists and turns in Life, so, when you *don't* have to be in a hurry, you can take the time to meditate. Only thing is there are times when you ARE in a hurry, so you need something to guide you. Well, you have that already, if you'll just think about it, and you don't even have to meditate about it. The Bible, silly willy, the Bible. It's right there in front of you. God has given that to us for guidance. It's our GPS! Isn't that wonderful?!?! Another wonderful is the GPS on your phone or in your car. In my early adult Christian life, there were times I didn't know where I was headed, but thankfully, I can now find my way around with both the Bible GPS and the GPS on my phone...Now and then, though, God's voice AND my phone's GPS can be heard saying, "Rerouting, rerouting ☺." (Oh, my, I took a wrong turn again...)

Today is Train Tuesday!

Today is TRAIN TUESDAY! We're not talking about a Choo-Choo ☺. (To form by instruction or discipline.) The focus from me today is that YOU can train yourself. No, not to be a Brain Surgeon, silly ☺. To help you become a better person. I can give you myself as an example. In Junior High we were required to read particular "classics," and I'm proud to say the "Blueblood ladies" (Google ☺) portrayed in those books helped to train me to handle situations in life as *they* did; maturely. Later, I read a powerful book about "positive thinking". All of the above, plus having a Christian upbringing, trained me to have a stable, functional, practical and mature outlook on Life. I knew that formal training wasn't an option for me, so I "trained myself to train myself." If you want to do better, you can. There are free "self-helps" for you everywhere today, if you choose to look for them. With all of that said, what I'm proudest of is that I trained myself to make it a habit to have Daily Devotions with the Lord. The Best Training I could ever give myself!

Today is Wrinkle Wednesday!

Today is WRINKLE WEDNESDAY! I imagine some of you ladies are already saying, "Oh, I can tell you about wrinkles, I have a few ☺." Well, I'll be the first in line to gasp about mine. I now tell folks, "They're not wrinkles anymore, they're absolute grooves ☺." Sooooo, we have wrinkles in the face, wrinkles in garments (Thank the Lord "Steamers" were invented! Don't know what I'd do without mine.) and then...and then...we have – ta-da! – wrinkles in our personalities. "Oh no," you're saying, "Let's not talk about those." Yes, we must, sorry. Every now and then we have to look at ourselves and iron out the wrinkles. The imperfections. Hey, don't let them get deeper! Get to it! The iron is hot. That means the Bible. It'll smooth out ANYthing you need smoothed. Wrinkles? No problem for The Word!

Today is Tag Thursday!

Today is TAG THURSDAY! (To hold to account.) Tag, you're it! Your turn! Does anyone "out there" remember that childhood game? It involves a player chasing other players in an attempt to "tag" (touch) them, which means they're then out of the game. Then the one that has been touched is the one who turns and passes it on – starts chasing everyone else, trying to tag them. Winner, of course, is the only one left in the game. Nothing complicated about it, but a lot of fun. Obviously, that was before the start of video games. When technology came about, it really progressed fast. Games of yesterday would be laughed at by most children in our present world. Today, though, as adults, we're going to play tag. Not really play, but put that game to work spiritually. Just one game-rule here: Be sure – sure – to pass on to your children, your relatives and friends, the importance of knowing where they're going when they leave this world. That's all I'm saying. I've tagged you. *Your* turn. Tag you're it! Now, pass it on.

Today is Flamboyant Friday!

Today is FLAMBOYANT FRIDAY! (Strikingly elaborate, colorful display or behavior.) Some ladies have told me that they always love to see what I'm wearing, which is usually Flamboyant. I claim to be "Modestly Flamboyant." Flamboyant – for me – is something that's pretty and "makes a statement" of class. I love to design my own clothes. My girls laugh because when I go into a fabric store, I just go "nuts" looking at all the material. Quickly designing in my mind. Fun, to me. My flamboyant behavior? Laughing a lot, of course ☺. Don't plan to do without it! When God designed the Tabernacle – and later the Temple – and its contents, He used Flamboyant colors, precious metals and jewels. What about that! A Flamboyant God. I love Him even more for being that! Flamboyant is fun!

Today is Self-Sufficient Saturday!

Today is SELF-SUFFICIENT SATURDAY! Do you need help with *any*thing today? I'm serious here. DON'T be like I was for many years. Self-sufficient, though I was a Christian, I didn't call upon God for ANYthing unless I absolutely had to. I loved God, Jesus and the Holy Spirit, but I figured I was supposed to do everything in life – that I could do – by myself. Did I pray? Yes, absolutely. But my prayer was always pretty much, "Lord, see me through this." And He did, of course. Several incidences in my life would've turned out better if I had not been self-sufficient. If I'd trusted God instead of myself. Some lessons are learned the hard way. I learned a few. After some of them, I'd say to God, "Lesson learned, Lord, lesson learned ☺." He probably leaned over the balcony of Heaven a lot, looking at me saying, "Just trust me, Laura, just trust me." Well, I FINALLY learned to trust Him. I'm surely NOT self-sufficient anymore (Well, not like I *was*☺,) and do I trust Him? Oh, my, not only that, I LEAN, folks. I *LEAN* on Him!!! I hope you'll learn NOT to be Self-Sufficient!

Today is Sovereign Sunday!

Today is SOVEREIGN SUNDAY! (A supreme ruler; possessing ultimate power; royal status; All of this=Our God). Thanks to our Heavenly Father, we have it all! When we have God and His Word in our lives, He's all we need, so we have it all here in America! We have Bibles to read. Can have fifty of them in our homes if that's what we want. Technology – available to anyone who wants it – to "reach out" across the world! Churches where we can walk through the doors to worship in sight of the police. Pass along the Good News ("The Four Gospels," Matthew, Mark, Luke and John) any way we choose to do it. We have it all! Thanks. to. our. Sovereign God. I repeat: You, my dear person, have it all...Thanks to your Sovereign God!

Week 36

Today is Mistakes Monday!

Today is MISTAKES MONDAY! Want to make a Mistake? I can tell you how to do that ☺, because I've made plenty in my time. There are little mistakes and big mistakes. Some, we can prevent, some we just plow into without thinking ahead, and then there are the ones which we know we're gonna make and don't try to stop. Those are the big ones. Some of us can tell you, "Don't do it! You'll wish you hadn't!" Years later you'll be saying, "Hindsight hurts." But if you're gonna do it anyway – even when somebody else tells you that you're making a mistake – be prepared for the consequences! They probably won't be good. Now: Just for today, let's see if we can go a *whole day* without making a "little" mistake, what about it! Can you work at it? The good thing is, when you make those little mistakes, at least you can laugh at yourself. I don't know what I'd do if I couldn't laugh at myself when I make a Mistake. Do you do that, too? Sometimes those little Mistakes can make cute memories...

Today is Touch Tuesday!

Today is TOUCH TUESDAY! Did you know you can touch God? The God that created the earth you're living on? Yes! You can! Go outside and touch a tree. Pick a flower. Pull up a blade of grass. That's the Hand of God! The *Face* of God! (Don't touch a wasp or a hornet, they might touch you back and it wouldn't be a fun time ☺.) God is everywhere! Touching Him is an awesome awakening, don't you think? And you want to know what else? God touches *you*! How? With the cool wind on your face, the warm sun on your arms, He's touching you with love. God loves touching you, my friend. Touch Him back...

Today is Wealthy Wednesday!

Today is WEALTHY WEDNESDAY! That's me! Wealthy! Bragging about it, too! And I share my wealth with thousands! "Wow, you must be really wealthy," you say. Yes, I am. See, I'm a Child of a King. He owns the cattle on a thousand hills, so I have all I ever need in life. I even have a mansion on another property, too, in Heaven, plus plenty of riches waiting on me there. Do I share my wealth with others? "You betchum, RedRider." (Google that and learn a bit of trivia from the 1940s.) Here's some of my wealth for *you*! Read John 3:16, do what it says, and voila! Instant wealth that YOU can then share with whoever you want. Get Wealthy!

Today is Today Thursday!

Today is TODAY THURSDAY! Funny subject, you may think. However, I just realized *this may be the most important Blurb that I ever write*! You see, we don't have yesterday. We don't have tomorrow. We only have Today. Today, friends. That's it. So, that means we have to make it count! Most important is to make sure you've accepted Jesus as your Savior. Then "line up with The Word." The Bible. That just means to do what it says. Every scripture. Not just the ones you like. As long as you're lining up the best you can, then you can be at peace Today. Tomorrow will get here when it gets here. Today is your focus. How to handle it? Simple. Live each hour as if it were your last. Today...is what matters. Think about it. *Today*.

Today is Feed Friday!

Today is FEED FRIDAY. We Feed ourselves to live, to keep up our energy. If we don't feed our body, we won't exist very long. But do we partake of spiritual food? If we don't feed our spiritual self, our heart, mind and soul will soon be empty! Now, go right this minute and get your Bible; put it in a spot where you can open it *any*time and Feed yourself. You'll start to really live!

Today is Subject Saturday!

Today is SUBJECT SATURDAY! (One that is placed under authority or control.) Every human alive is Subject under the authority and control of the Great I Am. God our Father. That's fine with me. Feels good to be His Subject! That means I'm on His mind. Every hour. Every day. Changing the "Subject," there have been times that I have been on someone else's mind because of an illness I was going through. Then, there have been many times when someone that I knew became the Subject of *my* thoughts and prayers because they were going through a bad time. Different days, different Subjects. If you're like me, probably your mind goes through a "ton" of Subjects during the course of a whole day. One of my favorite Subjects to think about is fun memories of Reunions. The Subject of conversation is likely to be, "Remember when your cousin threw you into the pond, then put you on the back of that pig ☺?" Memories are wonderful Subjects. Incidentally, Who's the Subject of your thoughts right now? Maybe it's a fun Subject!

Today is Swallow Sunday!

Today is SWALLOW SUNDAY! This is simple. Today we're gonna practice swallowing those words we were about to say in response to someone acting the fool. That sounds like good advice, I guess, but even I know at times it's not easy to keep that mouth closed. But do your best, okay, because I want to mention something else here about swallowing. As a citizen of this country, are you swallowing some of the things that our children are being taught at school today? Are you swallowing some of the laws that politicians are trying to pass? Friends, if ANYthing you heard does NOT line up with God's Word, then it's wrong. If you want God's favor on your life, you need to listen to Him, whether He's speaking in that still, small voice personally to you, or whether it's from your pastor or a good Christian friend. Swallow God's Word daily!

Week 37

Today is Memorable Monday!

Today is MEMORABLE MONDAY! (Worthy of being remembered.) Who in your life is worthy of being remembered? Perhaps it's a loved one already in Heaven. Perhaps a childhood friend you never kept up with after getting out into Life. Maybe a Teacher in High School that turned your path around when you needed better direction. What about The One that was beaten and crucified for you? Hmmmm? What about *Him*! Do you remember Him often enough? Daily? Friend, He's worthier than Anyone you'll ever meet! What? You haven't *met* Him??? Gracious! Get that Bible off your coffee table and turn to the Book of John and read the Story of the One who hung on the cross for us all! This will be the most Memorable day in your life when you make Jesus the Lord of your Life! *You'll* see...

Today is Transform Tuesday!

Today is TRANSFORM TUESDAY! Can you transform your feet into a different size? Nope. Impossible. Your hair a different color? Yep. Possible. But we're not gonna talk about physical things here, we're gonna talk internal changes. Transformation in the heart. In the mind. Attitude. Personality. Character. Question to yourself is, do you think anything in your life needs to be transformed from maybe a zero to a ten? Is someone else perhaps hoping you'll do some transforming? You don't have to transform yourself...*by* yourself. The God of the Universe won't force you to Transform, but He *will* help. He has the strength and the power. He's a gentleman, though, and will wait until you ask Him. Go ahead, He's waiting...

Today is Winning Wednesday!

Today is WINNING WEDNESDAY! I've "been there" with Life, so I'm qualified to tell you that you can make it through any given trial Life may throw you. It does take strength from the Lord Jesus, though, that's a given. My point is, when you read these daily Blurbs, rest assured they have slipped from my heart into the computer by way of Heaven. They're not words I decided to put down to fill up a page. Far from it. They're words of encouragement. As a songwriter, I've written "I'm A Winner Either Way," "Born to Win," and "I Can't Lose for Winning," so obviously I believe in winning! I KNOW you can come out on top of whatever you're going through in Life's Race... *IF* you choose to. Victory is waiting for you and winning is not a problem, as long as you do it with God as your Pilot. NOT Co-Pilot. You're the Co, He's the one at the wheel. Oh, you haven't let Him have the wheel yet? Well, no WONDER you haven't been Winning! Give it over to Him, N.O.W.

Today is Tumble Thursday!

Today is TUMBLE THURSDAY! (A gymnastic feat.) You may be one that can perform a gymnastic feat physically, but I'm not. Never could be one ☺. Jump rope, riding a bike and doing a somersault was about it for me, and that doesn't even come close to the gymnastic feats that are accomplished today. Well, let me correct myself; I *can* do the above Tumble. Yes, I can. Only one difference. Mine is mental. When I've done something that's totally embarrassing – usually in front of an audience – my mind does a flip, then tumbles across a mat, accomplishing a feat that covers my embarrassing moment. I scramble back up, quickly recovering from a workout ☺. My gymnastic mind-feat? It's called "Poking Fun." At my*self*. Don't know what I'd do without humor! So, Tumble Thursday? I tumble sooooo many other days, too! Might wanta call them "Fumble-Tumbles ☺." Can you Tumble, too?

Today is Fortunate Friday!

Today is FORTUNATE FRIDAY! How Fortunate we are to have this day at our fingertips! To thrive in, make conscious choices to renew different things we could do better, push on to finish the unfinished, and the list could go on and on. Most of all, how fortunate (blessed!) we are to know we can be in the palm of God's Hand. Are you there??? If so, you may sometimes drift off course, but you won't drift out of His Hand; so Fortunate.

Today is Seed Saturday!

Today is SEED SATURDAY! Here's the famous story of Johnny Appleseed (John Chapman, 1774-1845.) He was an American apple farmer who planted apple seeds across America. His dream was to produce so many apples that no one would ever go hungry. He always carried a leather bag filled with seeds he collected for free from cider mills. He planted them in open places in the forests, along roadways and by streams. He started this when he was only eighteen years old. What a harvest for the population back then! All from seeds planted. YOU can plant seeds yourself, today. Not apple seeds, but seeds of a different kind. My fellowman, you can spread seeds of the Gospel to those around you. In your conversations by merely including something like, "Look what the Lord made possible for me." This is a *great* Seed planted! YOU plant the Seed and God will do the growing!

Today is Supple Sunday!

Today is SUPPLE SUNDAY! (Readily adaptable to new situations.) We'd better be supple because Life has some curves we'll have to get around. Some mountains we'll have to climb. Some waters to swim through. Some deserts to cross. You'll wreck on the curves, fall off the mountains, drown in the waters, and die in the desert...unLESS you become Spiritually Supple. Friends, that *simply* means to "do" Life with two priorities in mind: (1) Read the Bible and do what it says, and (2) Do. It. In. GOD'S. Strength. Curves are possible to get around. Mountains are made to climb. Waters are made to swim/travel in. Deserts can be crossed. And, because you are Supple in your mind, heart and soul, you can do this! Hey, as a matter of a fact, you're DOING it! Yay!!!

Week 38

Today is Meaningful Monday!

Today is MEANINGFUL MONDAY! (Something one tends to convey.) I'm going to tell you how I found one of my favorite scriptures. Several years ago I decided to find a scripture "all my own" that isn't well known, like the Lord's Prayer, etc., to quote anytime an unwanted thought came. I found the perfect one, Psalm 51:10! It worked, too! Fast-forward...Lewis & Lewis were singing in North Carolina one weekend. After a Sunday morning service, I was relating my little "aggravating time" with the pastor's wife, and as I started quoting "my" verse from Psalm 51, *"Create in me a clean heart, O God,"* her husband, the pastor who was standing nearby, said with me, *"and renew a right spirit within me."* My mouth dropped open! I was astounded! I said, "That verse is well known?" He just laughed and said, "Yes!" I had to laugh, too, but the laugh was on me ☺. I was soooooo sure I had a scripture "all my own" that no one else paid much attention to. Was I ever wrong! Folks, maybe this scripture can be one of your favorites, too. It surely is good to quote when you're "less than" who you mean to be, because it'll make you feel "brand new." It's Meaningful...

Today is Temperament Tuesday!

Today is TEMPERAMENT TUESDAY! (Frame of mind as it affects a person's acts and words.) We've touched on attitudes, tones of words, etc., on other pages, but now let's get down to the nitty-gritty and use the real word. Temperament. Although we don't generally need to live our lives according to what people think of us, your life can be peaceful and smooth if your temperament is stable around other folks, especially ones you have close contact with. And if you don't care how you "come across" to others, shame on you. Even facial expressions can determine your temperament without your even saying a *word*. Raise your eyebrows in derision or sarcasm a lot? Don't. Quit it. Be nicer. "Why should I?" you ask. "Because I want to like you," I say, "and I can't if your Temperament is testy or negative consistently." So there.

Today is Watch Wednesday!

Today is WATCH WEDNESDAY! (Keeping awake to guard.) In the days of Cowboys and Indians and Outlaws (Not politically-correct nowadays, but that's what they were called from the beginning, so don't complain!), Pioneers had to keep watch and guard *constantly* just to stay alive. Today, we have just as many enemies to watch for, so I figure pretty much folks have watched for one enemy or the other since the beginning of Time. One enemy we ALL have in common – and I'll just use America here – from the Pilgrims to the Pioneers, to the 1900s when technology started to progress (electricity, automobiles, planes, phones), is the devil. Same devil that tempted Adam and Eve tempted your ancestors in every century, and he's still roaming through this world this very day! Watch out for him, *guard your heart and mind.* He'll be around soon enough. Hey! Why not be ready for him! Have some scripture in mind to quote – out loud – when he shows up. It'll send him packing! *Watch* and see!

Today is Tempest Thursday!

Today is TEMPEST THURSDAY! "Any violent commotion; a furious storm." I've had a lot of emotional storms in my life, so I can tell you from experience they're not fun. Though thunder rolled and clouds looked ferocious, the Lord held me in His Hand, keeping me close as my ship sailed the seas of life. Had it not been for God Himself keeping me safe till the storm passed by me, my sails would've been ripped into shreds. God is the opposite of stormy. He's full of peace. Stability. Will help you cope thru any Storm. Don't forget this when they come. Because they will.

Today is Fitting Friday!

Today is FITTING FRIDAY! (To put into a condition of readiness.) Are you getting Fit for battle? For sailing? For a camping trip? For Heaven? (Slipped that one on you, didn't I... ☺!) Listen to me, okay? If you lived back in the early centuries of Time, to prepare for battle you'd get fit with armor, etc. Heavy to wear. Even in today's wars our soldiers carry heavy loads. Still listening? Getting fit for sailing demands a life jacket for sure, plus a lot of other things. You have to plan for the unknown that can happen. You don't want to be caught unprepared. Same for camping. There's still wildlife to contend with in many areas of our country and you need to educate yourself on what can happen before you load your provisions, trek across the miles and set up your camp. Prepare. You know where I'm going with this, by now. Good. Here it is: Do you prepare for Heaven as meticulously as you do for Excursions on Earth? Hmmm? You know how, so don't say you don't. No heavy armor or military gear or life jackets or protection from wild animals needed. Just one item to carry. The Bible. That's it. Fitting.

Today is Shopping Saturday!

Today is SHOPPING SATURDAY! Shopping is such fun, especially for ladies. I've been extra blessed in that my husband loved to shop. He especially loved Flea Markets, Old Book Stores, etc. He always found some of the neatest treasures. When you go shopping, you not only can shop for shoes, clothing and accessories or whatever you're looking for, you can shop for opportunities. Opportunities? "What's that?" you say. Just what I said. Opportunities. That's one of my favorite things to shop for when I go to a store of *any* kind. I shop for someone to smile at, someone to make a comment to in the Produce section, for instance (commiserating about the price of this or that ☺), etc. Then when I check out, when the clerk says, "Have a nice (or blessed) day," though I used to say, "You, too," for a while now I've been saying – with a smile, "I already have!" I pass along my cheerful attitude, and Life is good! Next time you go shopping? Shop for Opportunities. Won't cost you a dime!

Today is Subtract Sunday!

Today is SUBTRACT SUNDAY! (Withdraw.) Take yourself away from people or situations that you know in your "gut" are not best for you. You're supposed to be a new man in Christ – better than you used to be – and old things are supposed to be passed away, so don't add unsavory things to your life...Subtract them! Just subtract them! Do it! (You had math in school...)

Week 39

Today is Meantime Monday!

Today is MEANTIME MONDAY! One "You" had plans to take a cruise. However, an illness was diagnosed and you have to do the surgery thing then recuperate. You still plan to take a cruise, but in the meantime, you have to get well. Another "You" has plans to be an engineer and you are just in your first year of college. You *so* look forward to the day when you'll have that degree. In the meantime, you'll be putting in a lot of hours of serious studying. Yet another "You" just went into the military for a few years. Gonna use that to get an additional education. It'll be a long stretch, but it'll be worth it. In the meantime, there are a lot of good things to learn. "In the MEANTIME," is verrrrry important. Probably the most important part of your journey, because that's when you learn many of life's virtues. Patience is one. Courage to continue and not stop is another. Push on. From a Higher View, Jesus said He'd be back for us and gave us signs to watch for, and it's about time now for Him to show up. However, "in the Meantime" scripture says we're to *"Occupy till He comes."* Lots of "Meantime" work still to do. Let's get busy!

Today is Tranquil Tuesday!

Today is TRANQUIL TUESDAY! (Free from agitation of mind or spirit, disturbance or turmoil.) You said you're not gonna let ANYthing keep you from having a peaceful day! Said you're determined. You decided that yesterday after dealing with problems that kept popping up. So, you've headed to get in your hammock and life's great already! Said you're just gonna enjoy it and that you're even gonna take a nap out there and rest. Said you deserve it because you realize that if you don't take care of yourself – meaning both mental and emotional strength – then you won't be in the best shape to take care of your loved ones. Now: *I'm* telling *you*...Who do you think made sure you can have this Tranquil day! It was the Holy Spirit, of course! MAKE SURE you thank Him for it. A Tranquil Day. My, my, sure love that word. (Hey, now I'm gonna have to go purchase *me* a hammock ☺.)

Today is Wakening Wednesday!

Today is WAKENING WEDNESDAY! (To rouse.) As children, most of us heard the story about the little guys who loved Snow White. You may identify with some of them, or know someone that does. For instance, I am kinda dopey upon wakening, but some folks wake up grumpy. My son, who went to Heaven at age nine, always woke up sleepy. I'd sit on the edge of his bed and gently "talk" him awake. That's a special memory for me. My daughter used to be called bashful. My nephew could be called Doc because he always has a "Natural" remedy for just about any ailment. Changing gears here, we adults are wakening to a whole lot of changes in today's world. Those changes are screaming at us. We can remain happy through it all though, IF we address the situation wisely and lovingly, by making sure our families and friends are Wakening with Spiritual Eyes. Let's get better at doing that! (Hey Y'all, we could be a Fairy Tale!)

Today is Treatment Thursday!

Today is TREATMENT THURSDAY! (Actions applied in a specific situation.) Are you gonna run roughshod over somebody today? Talk offensive to a clerk who only "works there," doesn't make the store's policies? Let's turn that around, okay? What if somebody's treatment of you is rude or offensive? In both instances, we need to be careful with our words *and* actions. A mentor once said to me, "Don't burn your bridges, you never know when you're gonna need to cross them again in the future." I've found that to be true, unfortunately. We've all heard the saying, "*What goes around comes around.*" That's the truth. And you know why? Because God is Omnipresent. That means He sees all and hears all. Bottom line, He's "Just." What "Just" means is simply..."*What goes around comes around.*" God's "Just" sees to it. So, my friends, be careful of your Treatment of someone, also how you react to someone's Treatment of you. Here's a thought: How's your Treatment of your Father? Your *Heavenly* Father…!

Today is Forever Friday!

Today is FOREVER FRIDAY! Wanta look younger? Wanta live longer ☺? Half of our population is always looking for that Fountain of Youth miracle. Well, guess what. It's not lost. It's been found for thousands of years. It's in a place called Heaven, and if you make it there, you're there for*EVER*! No ending of time. Not only that, you will neither have any wrinkles there, nor have to worry about getting any. Everything's perfect up there. Wanta go? I'm going. I can tell you how to get there. Pick up a Bible. Open it to John 3:16. Do what it says. Then, as far as the whole Bible goes...Read it, and *do* it! Are you prepared for FOREVER? Boggles the mind, doesn't it! When we cross over from this life to Heaven – those of us that are going there – that'll be the day we've been waiting for! Forever, here I come!

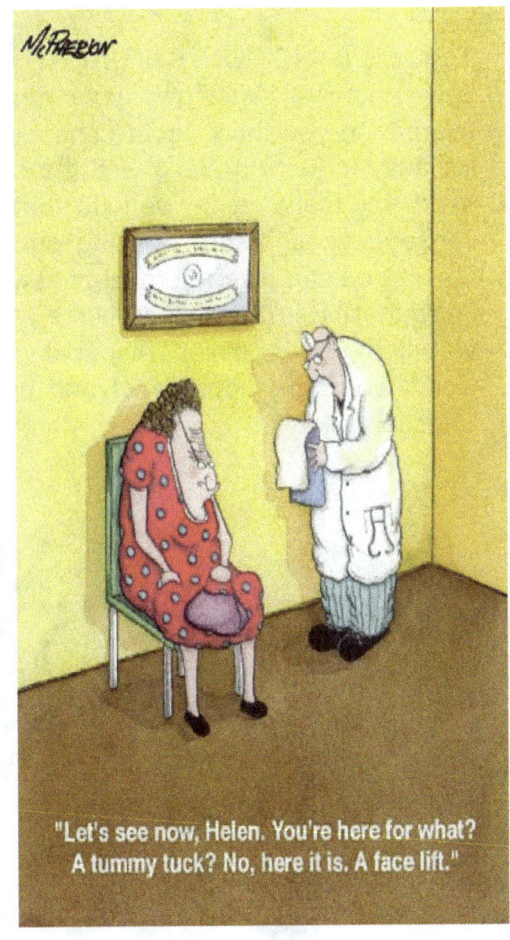

"Let's see now, Helen. You're here for what? A tummy tuck? No, here it is. A face lift."

Today is Sanction Saturday!

Today is SANCTION SATURDAY! (Give approval to; consent.) What do *you* sanction? What gets *your* approval? From daily happenings to big events, do you think about consequences before you give your consent? It's easy to just go along with the crowd on impulsive ideas, so we really need to make it a serious habit to quickly access any possible consequences before opening our mouth with a "Yes, I'll go along with that." You can give approval to something even with your silence, did you know that? Some people will take your silence for consent, since you're not verbalizing your opinion. Also, did you know that your very lifestyle tells the world what you approve of and consent to? Be very careful what you Sanction, okay?

Today is Ship Sunday!

Today is SHIP SUNDAY! *YOU,* my Friend, are a ship. Sailing on Life's Sea. Who do you have as your Captain at the helm? How you follow your compass (Bible) determines how you weather the storms. If you want to make it to the Harbor, you'd better ask Jesus to be that Captain. And I just happen to know He's available!

Week 40

Today is Magnificent Monday!

Today is MAGNIFICENT MONDAY! (Marked by stately grandeur, sumptuous in structure and adornment.) Thousands of pictures have been made of magnificent sunrises and sunsets, because they are magnificent. Same for the moon and stars, mountains, both stormy and peaceful seas, an oasis in the desert, etc. Man has been taking better care of these Wonders during the past few decades because of better equipment to help maintain our earth's visual treasures. Though some believe all of those magnificent things just evolved from nature's attributes through the ages, the real truth is a Living God fashioned it all. That's not all He did. He created something else magnificent. You. Yes, *you*. First of all, memorize Psalms 139:14. Then take a look in a mirror, and as you gaze, remember the verse. Do you see? You're wonderful and Magnificent! Did you know that? Wanta join me in taking better care of the temple (your body being the temple) God created, now that you know you're Magnificent?

Today is Tortoise Tuesday!

Today is TORTOISE TUESDAY! (Someone or something regarded as slow or laggard, lingers.) Do you remember the story about the Tortoise and the Hare? You *don't*? Where have you *been*! Just teasing, I know you're probably too young to have heard/read that ☺. Well, here it is: A Hare (rabbit) made fun of the Tortoise (turtle) for being so slow and challenged him to a race, thinking it was ridiculous for the Tortoise to even agree to the race, because he, the Hare, knew he was so much faster. He took off hopping, but after a short distance, decided he was so far ahead he'd just nap a bit. The Tortoise passed the sleeping Hare, plodding along slowly but steadily, and when the Hare woke up, the Tortoise was very close to the goal. Guess what. The Hare couldn't get there in time, no matter how fast he ran, and...he lost the race. So, folks? Being slow is not the worst thing at all. For instance, in reacting to people who are obnoxious, when you want to box their ears? Give it a second and react with a mature/wise "comeback" that makes them know they've lost the race. The Hare was too arrogant. Too prideful. The Tortoise was just laid-back. Which one are you, the Tortoise or the Hare?

Today is Weigh Wednesday!

Today is WEIGH WEDNESDAY! (To consider carefully in order to reach a conclusion.) When we use the word Weigh, the first thing we think of usually is our set of scales in the bathroom, telling us how many donuts we've eaten that we shouldn't have during the past month ☺. But today we're going to think about the scales in our minds. Yes, we do have those, and if you don't think you do, you need to create a set. That might mean a little maturing on your part. If you have any kind of decision to make in the near future – be it small or large – you need to weigh the pluses and minuses before you reach your conclusion. You can help yourself by making a list on paper to look at, or in your computer, on your phone, wherever. When you end up making the right decision, you'll know you weighed correctly. There's just *one* decision you need to make in your lifetime where you will *not* need to weigh anything. You see, there are only pluses, no minuses. When you make the decision to invite Jesus Christ into your heart and follow His leading for the rest of your life, the scales automatically Weigh in your favor! Incredible? You'd better believe it!

Today is Trial Thursday!

Today is TRIAL THURSDAY! I can add several other words to this one that'll describe part of our daily lives. Cares, woes, sorrows, problems and troubles. Want some more? Didn't think so. What about ol' Paul and Silas in the Bible; they sure had their share of trials, didn't they! Here's part of a song I wrote that tells what they chose to do during one trial: "*You gotta love Paul and Silas, they were in some pretty dire straits (Beaten, locked in jail). They could've been moaning and groaning; instead they began to praise. When you make the choice to glorify God, get ready to watch Him move. It worked for Paul and Silas and it'll work for me and you, too!*" (When they praised God, He shook the jailhouse, their chains fell off and they were free!) NOW PAY ATTENTION TO THIS VERSE: "*Life is all about choices, we make different kinds each day. Red shirt or blue, a truck or a Jeep, fried chicken or burger and a shake. No difference in our spiritual life, the same applies there, too. When Trials come, complain or praise, the CHOICE is up to you!!!*" (Folks, what's a little ol' Trial, when you have God on your side!) Whoohoo and yeehaw!

Today is Focus Friday!

Today is FOCUS FRIDAY! To me, there are different levels of Focus, and I have to write it from a Christian's point of view. You have your Main Focus, which is to keep God as your foundation in your daily life. When the Holy Spirit lives within you, most of the time you just automatically react spiritually to your thoughts and movements. Again, all of that is what I call your Main Focus. Then you have the Awareness Focus or what's going on around you, meaning whether you're crossing a street at the stoplight, eating with family or friends in a restaurant, driving on the interstate, or working on your job – whether it's as a housewife or working on an assembly line. Within your Awareness Focus, you constantly have your Future Focus. That's those "moment-thoughts" that cross your mind about what you're going to do after the 9-5 is over, what your plans are for the weekend, etc. In the midst of all of your focus, though, the Main Focus is at work, helping to influence and guide it all. My friend, as long as you keep the awesome Holy Spirit directing your day, it's gonna be a winner! By the way, I know you're focusing on reading this Blurb right this minute, but when you finish it, what's your Focus gonna be?

Today is Sashay Saturday!

Today is SASHAY SATURDAY! (Strut, glide in a conspicuous manner.) It's easy for me to sashay around the country wherever I go to sing, speak, or present a Songwriting Seminar, because I know I'm on the same page as everyone in the world. "What do you mean?" you say. "Everybody's different. You can't be on the same page as everyone in the world." I reply, "Yes, I can." Let me explain: It's true, we're all different in a lot of ways. One person likes their coffee black, and one takes it with cream. One votes for one party and their friend votes for another party. However, the one thing we have in common: Jesus Christ died for us ALL. We all fall onto the list of "all." No one is left out. He died for the one that likes coffee black, and He died for the one who likes cream in it. He died for every voter, no matter who they vote for. One Man died for everyone, and this puts us all on the same page. So, I'm on the same page as everyone else in the world. I qualify for Jesus' love. His salvation. His mercy. His grace, and I accepted it! What a deal! That's Sashaying grounds! Watch me Sashay ☺!

Today is Sunny Sunday!

Today is SUNNY SUNDAY! But, actually on the Sunday I'm writing this, the sun is not showing its "shine." The look of the day is gray/overcast. However, my eyes are capable of seeing the unseen because I choose to see from the heart, and what I see is a world filled with sunshine...The gray days – all of them – can shine for you, too, if you choose "Sunny" over gray! You can, you know.

Week 41

Today is Mannerly Monday!

Today is MANNERLY MONDAY! (Showing good manners, behavior bearing action or treatment.) Are you a Mannerly person? Better yet, have you taught manners to your children? From what many of us hear and see in supermarkets and restaurants, that teaching has been neglected. A boy who is "all-boy," as we say it, can still be just that and mannerly at the same time. To be mannerly is to respect. What about it, folks? Let's get back to mannerly ways, whaddaya say...Do your part; show/teach others, especially the young, how to be Mannerly. You can start today...if you *want* to.

Today is Tonic Tuesday!

Today is TONIC TUESDAY! (One that invigorates, restores or refreshes.) Is this you? I *thought* it was ☺! When you speak to someone with encouragement, they are refreshed. You can make a difference in someone's day by just a few good words, even of humor. When my husband and I first started seeing each other, he used to say things like, "You're just a little Hootenanny," (I made him smile and laugh) or "You're a Tonic for me!" I loved it! I was so glad that I refreshed him. I made a difference in his life. Showed him he could live Life with a zest! Are you a Tonic for the people in your world? You *can* be. Try it.

Today is Wash Wednesday!

Today is WASH WEDNESDAY! We Wash our feet. We wash our hands. What about washing our hearts and minds? Don't you just love that clean feeling when you've washed your hands and dried them? I love the kind of soap that smells good. (Most ladies will agree with me.) God's love is like that. It will make you feel clean, like you've been washed in the best smelling soap you can buy! How do you wash your mind? Make a list (be honest) of the things that you "know that you know." You don't need to be taking in things from the wrong kinds of books, television, movies, etc., so begin to eliminate those influences from your life. That is cleansing! Need help Washing? The Heavenly Father will be glad to help you. He can Wash *good*! Have you ever asked Him?

Today is Tiptop Thursday!

Today is TIPTOP THURSDAY! (Excellent, the highest point.) There have been a lot of Tiptop moments in the lives of most of us. As I write this, many zip across my mind, but the one that I know is at the tip of the top for me is when each of my babies were born, and in the first minutes of their lives, wrapped a fist around one of my fingers. What. a. moment. What a moment! It'll make your emotions soar to the top of the world! And, the best news is, there are so many Tiptop moments yet to come in Life, to savor, to place in the Memory Book of our hearts. We all truly have a lot to look forward to, if we'll just embrace Life. Tiptop moments...Wow.

Today is Fence Friday!

Today is FENCE FRIDAY! I've heard people say that if you don't stand for something in Life, you're susceptible for most anything. Lots of truth in that. Some people had rather sit on a fence because they don't want to admit which side of it they'd really prefer to stand on. Could be they're on that fence so they won't hurt someone's feelings, or cause an awkward situation for a friend, etc. I don't like to sit on a fence. It's not a safe, stable place to be. I could fall and be the one hurting, not someone else. I'd rather choose to get down from the fence and stand on the side that has the Best Ground to stand on. Are you sitting on a Fence about something? Sure seems to me like that would get to be pretty uncomfortable...

Today is Sublime Saturday!

Today is SUBLIME SATURDAY! (Outstanding moral worth; inspires awe because of elevated quality – like beauty or grandeur.) A lot of folks today make what's called a Bucket List. Things they'd like to do before life ends for them. I've never made one but if I did, one of the things I'd love to do is see all of the great scenic Wonders of the World. The highest mountain, the deserts, different seas, plus so much more. All these Wonders made by God Himself have to be so Sublime! Yet with all of these great wonders, when I pick a flower from a field or the woods and admire its beauty, though man tries to duplicate – and does a pretty fair job – there's nothing that can quite come close to the purity of what God has created/grown. If I had another lifetime to live here on earth, I'd make a lonnnnnng Bucket List ☺. I'd find flowers in different countries and enjoy it all because of Who created it. I insist on giving God the glory for everything created, whether it be the sublime Wonders of the World, man-made buildings or whatever, because He either did it Himself allowed it to form, or gave Man the knowledge to do it. *He's* Sublime!

Today is Sift Sunday!

Today is SIFT SUNDAY! To sift is to "sort out what is useful or valuable; examine critically." It's a time of the ages when we really need to get down to the business of sifting through our lives – making sure that our daily actions reflect what Jesus taught in the Word (Bible), and that when our end comes we're ready to meet The Creator with our hearts and lives as pure as we can make them! Need a Sifter? Bookstores sell lots of them!

Week 42

Today is Mystery Monday!

Today is MYSTERY MONDAY! Why is it a Mystery? Because you haven't lived through the day yet and it's a mystery right now as to what all is going to happen in your 24/7. You *think* you know, but you really don't. Remember all the times you made plans and the whole day turned out different? Well, that could happen today as well, and you know it. Listen to this: "*We open our eyes to dawn's misty light, not knowing what the day has in store, maybe sunshine and gladness or heartache and sadness awaits just outside the door. But we need not fear for Grace will be there to meet us and lead us on through, and in each situation, trial or temptation, it's always amazing what God's Grace can do!*" That's a verse to the song I mentioned in Week 14, Fresh Friday." It talks about God's Grace being fresh every morning! Isn't that awesome? So, though you may not be able to count on a day going as you planned, you *can* count on God's Grace seeing you through whatever *does* happen. *So* comforting! No Mystery about that.

Today is Trawl Tuesday!

Today is TRAWL TUESDAY! (A large net dragged on the sea bottom in gathering fish.) You're probably thinking, "What does the word Trawl have to do with me? I'm not a Fisherman." Are you a Christian? Yes? Then you're a Fisherman and your Trawl (net) is the Gospel. Matthew 4:19 says, "*And he saith unto them, "Follow me, and I will make you fishers of men*." Now, I know you can't drag men like a real net, but your trawl can entice men to be introduced to Jesus. They'll never be sorry you brought them to meet Him! He's easy to love. By the way, have you caught any fish lately???

Today is Walk Wednesday!

Today is WALK WEDNESDAY! As you get ready to walk through your day, you may be weighed down with a problem either physical or emotional, or even both. It may feel like you're the only one that's ever been through what you're dealing with, but that's not true. I want you to read this verse: *"I've spent some time strolling around Peaceful Circle and I love taking walks to Joyful Street, but I've cried long hours of bitter disappointment on a highway full of potholes named Defeat. I've stumbled dejected down a road called Discouraged, stood broken on Heartache Avenue; then my Roadmap showed the entrance to Hallelujah Freeway, Praise God I reached it and I walked that mile, too!"* See my friend? You're not alone walking those difficult miles. MANY before you have walked the same miles! So, today? Make sure – no matter where you go – your Walk includes Jesus!

Today is Triumphant Thursday!

Today is TRIUMPHANT THURSDAY! (Victorious, celebrating, successful.) You're Triumphant because you learned there's someone that listens totally to you, as if you're an important person. And you *are*, to Him! It's your Heavenly Father. It's so good to know He listens to your every word! In days gone by, you met with groups who were discussing plans, etc., and though you tried to grab a moment to say a few words, nobody would give you a chance because they were so busy talking without stopping. Later when you were telling the Lord how discouraged it made you feel, the silence of His listening made you realize, "He's listening to me! Letting me talk!" And you've been so happy and triumphant about that! Not only that, you haven't stopped talking to Him all the time since then, either ☺, and you *know* He loves that! Oh, what a Triumphant Thursday!

Today is Fitness Friday!

Today is FITNESS FRIDAY! Fitness is *NOT* just for the body; it's for the mind and the spirit as well! "Fit for what/who?" you may ask. It's for your destiny as well as folks around you! If you're fit, you can make a difference in others. The Good Lord gives lots of "helps" to make good fitness possible plus to keep fit as long as we want! One help is that famous scripture I've already mentioned on other pages that says, "*I can do all things thru Christ Jesus which strengthens me.*" (Phil. 4:13.) How Fit are you?

Today is Seesaw Saturday!

Today is SEESAW SATURDAY! Remember the Seesaw on the playground in school? What fun! Kinda taught us how to react to the Game of Life that sends us up, then down, upon occasion. Too soon we discovered this adult seesaw wasn't fun like the one in the Park. But you've learned about Life's seesaws and how to make it all work without whining (You *have*, haven't you?), so all is well. You finally realized the great blessing of the seesaw of daily living is to "ride it" spiritually. As your trust in the Lord goes up, your fears and cares of Life go down. You've shown you can ride that seesaw like a pro now ☺. All it takes is "growing in the Lord." Hmmm, think I might call a friend, go find a playground and Seesaw a while ☺. Up and down, up and down. (Oops, getting dizzy just thinking about it. Might just as well stay home ☺.)

Today is Share Sunday!

Today is SHARE SUNDAY! What do you share? If you're a man, you might share tools from your garage shelf or your shop. A lady has fun sharing recipes. My daughters and I share clothes. What about sharing your time doing something for someone less fortunate than you – just because you can. Do any of you share that? One of the best things you can share is...yourself. Share your heart. Today, I'm going to share something I've never shared before – my family's motto. I've been proud of it ever since my childhood years when I learned it goes way back to my ancestors centuries ago. It's simply, *"Everybody's business is nobody's business."* That taught me to respect the privacy of everyone else. Now it may become your family's motto...Pass it on. Share it. I just did.

Week 43

Today is Melodious Monday!

Today is MELODIOUS MONDAY! (Having a pleasing melody.) Have you ever heard the ocean "sing?" It sings of life swimming underneath, of tumultuous waves making their own melody, and of countries on the other side of it full of Brothers and Sisters in Christ you've never met. Yes, the ocean "sings." What about mountains with their grandeur humming a low bass that calls peace to your soul, their gentle breezes singing a soft tune, the cracking sounds their rocks make, adding percussion to it all? Yes, the mountains "sing," too. Sweet sounds. Sweet living. Isn't Life great!?! What about you, my Friend; does your Life sing? Does your character give off a melodious tune? What kind of tune? Low-key rumbling? High screeching? Or a nice, easy-listening Melodious sound...

Today is Transcend Tuesday!

Today is TRANSCEND TUESDAY! (To rise above or go beyond the limits.) Do you go beyond the limits for your family? Most good people do. Do you transcend from flat to flavor, meaning from a slug to a salt-of-the-earth person? Great! You've transcended well! What about when your time comes to go to Heaven, will you be able to look back and feel you've been the person you know you should've/could've been? Examine yourself and make sure. If not, get busy on that word, Transcend. That's what Jesus did for *you*. He went *waaaaay* beyond the limits. Still does, my Friend, still does....

Today is World Wednesday!

Today is WORLD WEDNESDAY! Who's in *your* world? There's a different world – as we call it – in the mind of every human, even as we all live on this earth together. Your *world*, though, consists of everything that's in your mind. Your memories, everything you can remember until right now, your plans, dreams, your friends, loved ones, where you're going, what you're doing, all of it. *That's* your world. Some peoples' "worlds" encompass more people, more endeavors, bigger areas than others. For instance, my world includes a lot of folks who hear my music, contact me, etc., in comparison to other folks who might not care to have Internet, etc., just go to church on Sunday, and that's their world. I think you understand what I'm saying here. Now, I want to ask you: Is God and His Master Plan in your world? If not, today could be a brand-new world for you, one that would take you eventually to *another* world called Heaven. And Friend, you *do* want to go to *that* world, trust me! Trust your Heavenly Father! Make sure you go to *His* World!

Today is Triple Thursday!

Today is TRIPLE THURSDAY! (Three times as great or as many.) As a child I was raised to know all about God and His Son, Jesus. However, I didn't learn about the precious, awesome Holy Spirit until I was in my late teens. I suppose I "heard" the words at some point but being young, they didn't register. Isn't it wonderful that we have God in Triple, so to speak? I'm thankful God sent His Holy Spirit to us here on Earth. To comfort us. He's God present within us, making "moves" for us. He brings things to our attention, like a discrepancy on something you're about to purchase. Warns us of danger. Slows us down because he knows there's a cop ahead, for instance. He's Pretty Special! As God's children, we as Christians (Christ-like) are most blessed! Triply blessed! Love you, my Heavenly Father, my Lord Jesus, and Sweet Holy Spirit!

Today is Flow Friday!

Today is FLOW FRIDAY! Like most, I want to feel I've done some good with my Life's work. Even though we may feel a peace from the One Above about our life's work, still after a while it's great to have a human let us know that some of our words flow into the minds and hearts of someone; to know they mattered enough to cause even one person to make better choices, to grow in character. To grow in the Lord. Do your words or actions flow through you to others and perhaps influence them to make positive changes in their ways? See if you can make that happen. Starting Today. FLOW, my fellow person, FLOW!

Today is Still Saturday!

Today is STILL SATURDAY! Although I've had to do it many times in my life, I've never been tickled to arise in the mornings before daylight. And, I'm always surprised at the number of folks that tell me they LOVE getting up then, just so they can experience the Still/Quiet of that time of the morning (To me it's still "night ☺.") They love communing with God during those early moments of the day. There are a lot of scriptures that refer to this Still/Quiet time, so I know it must be special to God. Here are some for you to read: Psalms 46:10, 37:7, 62:5, Exodus 14:14, Isaiah 32:17, Ecclesiastes 3:7, James 1:19, and Job 6:24. If you're an EMP, I applaud you! (Early Morning Person.) (Note: My heart and mind love the Still/Quiet time of the early mornings, I just cannot convince my sleepy body to love it, as well ☺.)

Today is Smart Sunday!

Today is SMART SUNDAY! Millions of people in this world are intelligent, and that's a good thing. But if they don't ask Jesus to come into their hearts, they might be intelligent – but they're not SMART (means "quick to learn"). Takes a smart person to know what's good for them. How smart are *you*??? Is your name written in the Lamb's Book of Life in Heaven? If so, now *that's* Smart!

Week 44

Today is Matchless Monday!

Today is MATCHLESS MONDAY! We all have outstanding moments in our lives, which we'll never forget. They're Matchless. One of mine I wouldn't trade for anything happened when I was thirty years old. That's when I turned my FIRST problem completely over to the Lord so He could take care of it. Thirty years old! That doesn't say much for my "growing in the Lord," does it! For goodness sakes, I'd been a Christian since I was saved at age seven. Yet I'd never allowed Him to have the whole "job." Well, guess what! He came through for me! It was a heartbreaking problem that I gave to Him one Sunday morning. The following Thursday, I received a phone call that ended heartbreak. Total God at work! What *wonder* I had for my Heavenly Father! It changed not only that situation, it changed *ME*!!! I've been turning my troubles over to Him ever since! Growing in Him. Now I anticipate what He's going to do for me when I give Him my cares. What he did for me that day was a Matchless event for me because of His Matchless Love for me! Hey, He'll do the same for you! Let Him. Go ahead, give Him your burdens!

Today is Tiptoe Tuesday!

Today is TIPTOE TUESDAY! (To proceed quietly or cautiously.) Are you going to Tiptoe through the day or are you one of those people who believe they have to *trample* their way with every step? You can't respect someone that brusquely tramples, now can you! And you want to be respected – instead of dreaded – so keep on Tiptoeing. It simply means to be cautious – even as you stride steadily through life with your chin up, confidence in your eyes, and your shoulders straight. *There* you are! I see you coming, though I don't hear you...because you Tiptoe. Thanks. I appreciate that. Others do, too.

Today is Wonder Wednesday!

Today is WONDER WEDNESDAY! (Like a new experience; a cause of astonishment or admiration.) I have to tell you about one of the biggest Wonders I've ever experienced, and it was while I was nearing the end of writing this book. I was doing my morning Devotions, sitting at my Dining Room table. I'd just read something about how God is omnipresent, and in imagining that, I looked up from my book intending to just look around me, and what happened was – I looked across the table at God!!! Obviously, I didn't see His real face. But He was "sitting right there" and it hit me like a ton of bricks, as we say. There He was. My gaze included my kitchen because of where I was sitting, but folks, all of that was in the background. Though I was looking at air, I was looking at God, and I knew it. The God of all – the sun, moon and stars, universe – was sitting across the table from me! It was earthshaking. It was thrilling. It was humbling. It was awesome. I could "see" such love in His eyes. What a Wonder it was for me! Hey, why don't you try looking *at* "Him," as if He's sitting right there with you, *because He is*! It'll change your perception of Omnipresent. It'll be a wonderful, marvelous, incredible Wonder for you!

Today is Thoughtful Thursday!

Today is THOUGHTFUL THURSDAY! (Absorbed in thinking, heedful anticipation of needs of others.) Do you offer to punch the correct-floor button on the elevator for someone that just got on? Open the door of a store and allow folks behind you to go in first? Do chores for the Widow on your block or Widower up the street? Volunteer for different jobs at church? Wash or clean your aging parents' car? Clean the coffeepot at work? If you do any of the above, then you'd probably do them all, if the situation fits. That means you're a considerate individual. God bless you for that. God bless you greatly. Many people appreciate you, Thoughtful Person!

Today is Faith Friday!

Today is FAITH FRIDAY! Without faith, it's impossible to please God. What?!? You didn't know you were supposed to please Him? That's a scripture you're supposed to learn in your spirit. God honors Faith. He heals our broken bodies, broken spirits, broken finances, broken marriages or relationships and broken hearts. If you have any of these, just open your heart and talk to God about it. Tell Him how you feel, what you need. *Then* step out on Faith and believe. Believe He will do it. Expect. To expect it to happen is a form of exercising your faith, of letting it "work." There are several verses in the New Testament about Faith, so if I were you, I would go to my Bible and look them up. Quicker is to google "Verses in the Bible about Faith." When you finishing reading them, you'll see that if you're using your Faith, you're pleasing God. And you *want* to please Him because you're His child. So, make sure you act like it.

Today is Sufficient Saturday!

Today is SUFFICIENT SATURDAY! The Bible says that God's Grace is sufficient for us. That means for any situation. We'd be in a heap of trouble if we didn't have Grace. So, after you read this, why don't you go to your Bible and look it up for yourself. A song of mine: "*Don't take my word for it. Take His!*"

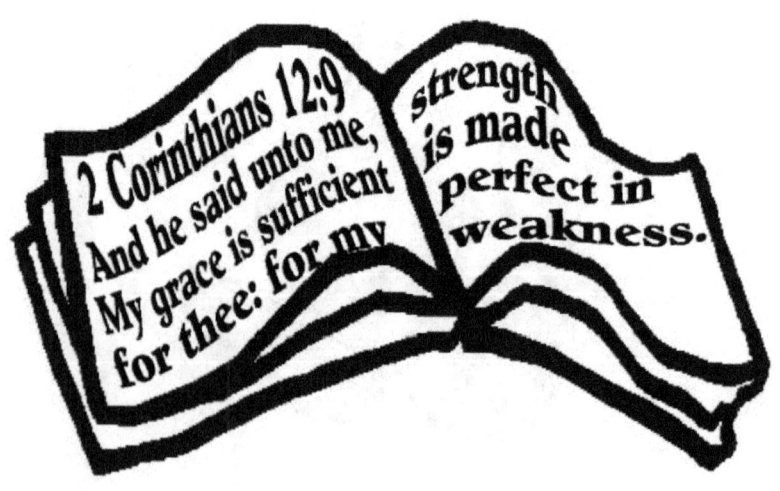

Today is Step Sunday!

Today is STEP SUNDAY! When you leave high school or college, you're usually ready to take giant leaps into the world. Hurry and make a difference in this thing or that. Nothing wrong with your attitude. Then, when life takes a different direction than what you'd planned, okay, you just take a step at a time until you're comfortable with where you're going. Same destination, just a different vehicle. Life is like an adventure, if you'll let it be just that. Don't let it stress you. Take one step at a time. Don't try to strain your life-muscles by (1) choosing a destination with too many steps to climb for your peace of mind, taking the joy of living away from you, or (2) by taking two steps at a time instead of one, missing something important life could show you. Years ago I learned to pray, "Heavenly Father, I trust you to show me where to put my foot down next." Best Step I ever took...Which direction is your next Step headed?

Week 45

Today is Model Monday!

Today is MODEL MONDAY! Who do you Model your life after? Your father? Uncle? Brother? Your Pastor? A Movie Star? Clark Kent? (Had to slip that in there ☺.) Your Boss? Nothing wrong with any of that IF they're good role models. If they're not, you may be in trouble. The Lord knows we need some better ones in today's world than those who seem to be prevalent. Where are our John Waynes and Paul Harveys!!! Obviously, it goes without saying that Jesus is the Best Role Model we could EVER pattern our lives after! Now, *who* did you say you pattern your life after??? (Louder, please, can't hear you).

Today is Tow Tuesday!

Today is TOW TUESDAY! Some marriages are such that one spouse is like a tugboat, pushing, pulling and Towing the other one toward different goals – to have a stronger marriage, to become more stable, and the list goes on. Though a tugboat doing what it does – towing – plays an important part for ships, boats, barges, and water travel, being a human tugboat is not only stressful and no fun, it's an out-of-balance situation, obviously. Why not enlist the help of the best Tugboat known? Jesus Christ! Now *He* gets the towing done! He puts everything back into balance. No more being a Tugboat for you, and no more pulling or pushing. You won't have to Tow anymore! Call on Jesus. Just *do* it!

Today is Well Wednesday!

Today is WELL WEDNESDAY! Saved when I was seven years old. Couldn't understand the next day at school why teacher wouldn't let me line the class up and have Testimony Service ☺. (I was used to Testimony Service at our church, so I thought it would be good for school, too ☺.) Christ's "Well of Living Water" was springing up in my little heart and I wanted everybody else to feel it, too. Waited till "Playtime" and lined 'em up outside and had my service anyway ☺. Through all Life's hurdles, my Well (soul) has never been diseased. Today, my Well is still well. What's in *your* Well?

Today is Torch Thursday!

Today is TORCH THURSDAY! (One definition is "A slang word that means to beat an opponent in a humiliating way.") This might be the day you decide to "Torch" the devil! You know he needs it! He's working overtime in the world today because he knows his time is short. Do you know he can read? *Sure,* he can! He knows the Bible from the first verse to the last. He's mentioned in it many, many times! He's out to destroy you and yours. Don't trust what *I* say, read the book and see for yourself. How do you Torch the devil? Just use the name of Jesus, Friend. That's it. Study the Word. Become spiritually educated, why don't you...Any reason why you can't???

Today is Fortitude Friday!

Today is FORTITUDE FRIDAY! (Strength of mind that enables one to bear pain with courage.) Where does Fortitude come from? Different places. It can come from being raised with teaching on how to have strength of mind, it comes from the Lord, and from choosing to be strong. When you get knocked down in life, bouncing back up will help you develop Fortitude, and here's part of a song Ray, my husband, wrote that might remind you to bounce. (If you're a Christian, you'll appreciate it more). "*We all get bounced around traveling down the road of life, So, don't think it strange when everything goes wrong instead of right. The road we travel is straight and narrow but it ain't no Primrose Lane, There's big chug-holes that'll jar your soul and test your spiritual springs...So, bounce back up like a rubber ball when life knocks you down, When you get hit, don't faint or quit and don't just roll around on the ground. It does not take brilliance to see resilience: is a necessary trait Like it or not, we're gonna bounce a lot between here and the pearly gates...?*" Have you bounced this year? If so, is your Fortitude getting stronger? Hope so!

Today is Situation Saturday!

Today is SITUATION SATURDAY! (Critical, trying or unusual state of affairs.) So.....you have some situations you've been dealing with for a while and you're really tired of them wearing you down...Is it anger? Bitterness? Hurt? Jealousy? Or maybe you're just plain lonely. You've hidden this satisfactorily, though, you think. Well, think again. You haven't hidden it from *every*body. You don't hide ANYthing from your Heavenly Father. He knows your every thought and all your emotions. He can take that problem of yours and zap it into nothingness, and then the emotion you'll be left with...is PEACE! You need to know that God is used to Situations like yours. He's dealt with zillions of them – just like yours – down through the ages of Time. Go ahead...let Him zap your Situation.

Today is Substitute Sunday!

Today is SUBSTITUTE SUNDAY! Lots of things to Substitute positively. A salad or fresh vegetables instead of burger and fries, a used car instead of a new one that would overload you financially, thrift and discount stores for certain items instead of charging at an upscale department store, home games with the family instead of partying, church on Sunday instead of going to the river. You understand what I'm pointing out, don't you? Now: Just turn each of those examples around and you'd be substituting negatively. You don't want to do that! (Do you? And if you do, WHY!) No matter what you choose in your life, the most important thing to always remember is: God will never be a Substitute. You either choose Him...or you don't. No Substitute for Him. Do you know that? Do you???

Week 46

Today is Mold Monday!

Today is MOLD MONDAY! (Distinctive character, to shape, to fit the contours of, i.e., a man of austere mold.) God creates us, and as we grow into adulthood, He begins to mold us into something that'll be good for us. Sometimes we resist being molded. Sometimes it hurts. But the molder knows His clay – you and me – and knows what it takes to shape us into the awesome mold He's planned for each one of His children. He molds us tenderly and lovingly because He can see the end result of what He's molding us to be. Today being Mold Monday, be thankful to your Molder for His powerful hands that mold, and His love for you that guides His hands. *Love Him back.*

Today is This Tuesday!

Today is THIS TUESDAY! Yes, *This* Tuesday. This Tuesday's for you! Not *next* Tuesday. This is a different Tuesday than you've ever lived before, so you should approach it with anticipation of all *kinds* of good things you can make happen. What can you do to make *this* Tuesday special? Think Positive now, don't go negative on me by assuming it's gonna be just "another" day. It *will* be, though, if you *allow* that. But since you have a good mind, use it to come up with at least *one* thing to make *this* Tuesday a better day than – say – yesterday was. For instance, maybe you can start learning to play guitar today! Your son knows how and could teach you some chords. Also, you usually just pray once in the morning and once at night? Hey, adding even a prayer in the middle of the day is different. And it would be special to God. See there how easy it is to make THIS Tuesday different? (Now you can start thinking about next Tuesday. Just kidding, just kidding ☺...)

Today is Wary Wednesday!

Today is WARY WEDNESDAY! Means "careful; aware." If you're careful *and* aware, your chances of being hit by a wayward vehicle are lessened. Thus, we can parallel this to our lives. Watch for trouble coming *and* avoid it. Detour around those areas where you know it's most likely to be. Most of all, detour around the spiritual enemy...namely that ol' devil! When you see him coming, be Wary and head in the opposite direction. That would be to Jesus, whom the devil is verrrrry Wary of! Good move for you!

Today is Trouble Thursday!

Today is TROUBLE THURSDAY! Watch for it, because it's bound to show up! Troubles happen because they are both an unfortunate and unfavorable circumstance that our Heavenly Father either allows to happen – or even sometimes brings forth in our lives – to help us "grow" our faith. Importantly, they're not to sink our ship. God's concern is (1) HOW you react to your troubles and (2) IF you've grown in trust and faith when you've landed on the other side of those troubles. He'll see you through them, even if you've caused them yourself. If you can ever "get it" in your spirit that God *loves* you and only wants the best – *His* best – for you, and TRUST Him with your Life, your every step, then any trouble that comes your way from that point can only make you grin. Smile. I'd rather have a life filled with Trouble and know that the Only Living God of this Universe loves me, than to live a smooth life with no problems and *not* have His Love! TROUBLE? Means God loves you!!!

Today is Farewell Friday!

Today is FAREWELL FRIDAY! The Bible says we'll have trouble here on earth in our lives, but we know there's a better place waiting for us! One day we'll say Farewell to cares and troubles. Farewell to sickness and illness. Farewell to evil. Goodbye to temptation of any kind. Goodbye to all the "dis" things we go through: disappointments, dissolutions, disapproval, discouragement, dismay, etc. Goodbye to old age and wrinkles ☺. When? The moment we leave this earth and say Hello to St. Peter at the Gate. Wow, we have a lot of perfection to look forward to in Heaven, don't we, and many of us already have loved ones already there who said Farewell to Earth's life, then embraced Paradise! Don't you *know* they're having a grand time!?! Now: I'll never be able to meet all of you who are reading my book, but if you've made sure you're going to Heaven when you say Farewell here, I'll see you there!

Today is Style Saturday!

Today is STYLE SATURDAY! Talking about Fashion here, so basically the ladies will pay more attention than the men, I imagine. Understandable ☺. This is just a tip, an FYI, okay? As a teen aware of fashion, I longed to be in style. A Minister's daughter with four brothers and five sisters, we were always the recipients of boxes and boxes of clothes from well-meaning people. But you can guess; most garments were out of style. Becoming creative, I took full (gathered) skirts off their waistbands, and cut out "straight" skirts or dresses that were in style. After marriage, I continued sewing because I loved to design, and made clothes for my children as well. But ladies, by my thirties I'd learned one important thing; if a garment made me look good, then I considered it MY style. No, this Blurb isn't especially spiritual, but maybe it will speak to someone who doesn't feel secure if they're not dressed fashionably. If it makes you look good, wear it! Guess what. It won't matter a hundred years from now if you've been in style or not. All that will matter is if your name was written in the Book of Life. Now, that's Style! Your name in that Book!

Today is Study Sunday!

Today is STUDY SUNDAY! Are you a people-watcher? Do you study them? It's fun. Educational. Actually, as you pass them in the supermarket, it's something you do without thinking about it. But here's a fact you DO need to think seriously about...Be careful how you live, because your children and grandchildren – and greats – will. want. to. live. like. you. do. Is that a good thing from your point of view? Know one thing: God is VERY aware of how you treat and raise the little ones; watching your every move. He expects you to Study His instructions (Bible) and rear your children accordingly. If you haven't read those scriptures, today would be a good day to look them up and Study them. Okay?

Week 47

Today is Mellow Monday!

Today is MELLOW MONDAY! (Means made gentle by maturity.) Some say as we grow older, we "mellow out." That's because we've learned that sometimes what we thought were mountains were only hills. There's a lot of stress in plain living today, so if we can "mellow out" there's less chance of a heart attack or stroke. Let me present the one who can help with "Mellow". Oh, you already guessed. Yes, it's the One and Only...God.

Today is Testament Tuesday!

Today is TESTAMENT TUESDAY! The New Testament of the Bible starts with Matthew, Mark, Luke and John, called the Gospels. Meaning the Story of Jesus. I call it the Old, Old Story. Two thousand years old. Most believe it. Some don't/won't. They believe what they read in most any educational book, but not the book that's proved to be the most accurate one in existence. More than sixty renowned scientists believe the Bible is true and that God did create all the Heavens you can see with your mortal eye, plus a lot more only astrologers see. But another truth? His *greatest* creation...is you. Psalms 139:14 says, "*I will praise thee; for I am fearfully and wonderfully made: marvelous are they works; and that my soul knoweth right well.*" Aren't we awesome? Created intricately by God! Though I love reading different stories in the Bible, knowing they're true, *nothing* surpasses the story of Jesus in the New Testament. His story holds the key to what happens to YOU when you leave this world. If you haven't read it, you need to get started, Friend...!

Today is Wet Wednesday!

Today is WET WEDNESDAY! Meaning rain. When rain wets the ground, it nurtures and makes/helps things grow and flourish. Are you growing in the Lord/Word? Your Bible is rain incognito. Wet my mind, Lord.

Today is Tweak Thursday!

Today is TWEAK THURSDAY! (To alter; improve by making fine adjustments to it.) Have you ever been to a live concert? Could be Pop artists, Country or Gospel. Whatever. Before the concert, they set up a sound System and test it over and over, to make sure the vast audience can hear every word. It takes tweaking a lot of knobs and slides to get the right sound for a particular building/atmosphere. Just thinking about that, I figure God sometimes has to tweak our minds and hearts to make sure we hear exactly what He's saying, cause whatever it is, it's gonna be important and something we need to hear. I wish I were perfect so He wouldn't have to tweak me, but I'm not. I've been tweaked by Him before many times. Can you hear what He's trying to tell you? Do *you* need Tweaking?

Today is Figure Friday!

Today is FIGURE FRIDAY! (Calculate or work out.) In Figuring the intricacies of Life, how to live, how to make it, attitudes, relationships, work, etc., have you figured out how to Love? I'm speaking of the Love that God intended us to have for our fellow man. Throughout the Bible, He commands us to Love. He also says that unless we Love, all our works are in vain. So, we'd better get that right, don't you think? How do we do it successfully? If you can give of yourself and expect nothing in return, if you can forgive others who've judged you wrong, if you see a hungry child and want to take care of it as you do your own, if you can give the Lord the Glory for all the works you've accomplished, then you are doing great at learning to Love as God intended. How to Figure Love? Ask Him.

Today is Savory Saturday!

Today is SAVORY SATURDAY! (Pleasant to the mind/taste; enjoy, to delight in; relish.) I don't know about you but I love to eat. There aren't many foods I dislike. I enjoy ice cream a lot more when I remind myself that our ancestors – in many climates across the world – didn't even know what it was. They missed out. So, I eat enough for them, too ☺. What about soft drinks/pop, as we call them. Basically, folks in centuries before ours only had fruit drinks, then eventually tea and coffee. Aren't we blessed! Hey, be thankful for every little savory morsel you eat, because (1) not only are there hungry folks in the world that would LOVE to have the foods we do, as I've pointed out before, (2) God could've created you and me in the 1300s, etc. and we would've missed out on the yummy ice cream of Today, in the summertime ☺. But we're *here*! With awesome ways to cook delicious foods quickly. We don't have to stand over an open fire. We all need to be thankful that we have such a great life! I'm afraid we take a lot for granted. What do you think? I love my Heavenly Father for putting me in this day and age, and I thank Him regularly for that. Today, let's enjoy each Savory bite we swallow ☺!

Today is Same Sunday!

Today is SAME SUNDAY! This word is very powerful when you put it in the context of all the changes that have taken place in our country, our world, during the past few years. It can really ruin your day if you spend too much time thinking about it. Yes, we need to be concerned. Pray for our Leaders as the Word tells us to do. However, I love to focus on the "big picture." That's just this: IF you believe in God, then you should believe that He has everything under control. He really does. We change, but He doesn't. It's pretty simple: We let *Him* do the work, and *we* do the trusting! Trusting Him to take care of us through all the hard times. Through the changes. And He will. You see, He's the Same yesterday, today and forever! So, I for one just hold on to His unchanging Hand! Always the Same. I love that word. Same. Same God Abraham, Moses, David, Daniel, and all the rest of the folks in the Bible trusted. Same one. Pretty incredible!

Week 48

Today is My Monday!

Today is MY MONDAY! Yep, it's yours. Totally. Although God is in control of EVERYthing in the world, including *you*, He gave you free will so you can choose to do anything that you can make happen. So. You WILL be choosing how your day goes, one way or the other. You're an adult, so you already know there are consequences from every choice made, be it large or small. Like, go to work? Or not. Change the oil in your car because it's already a few hundred miles over the limit? Or not. If you're leaving work, are you gonna go home or hang out in a bar with some buddies? *FROWN* all day at everybody you meet because you're ill at yourself because you know you're making wrong choices? Or *SMILE* because you're happy that you're using the free will YOUR CREATOR gave you – trusted you with – to mature with life; to be thankful God loves you. Not only *that,* to realize He believes in you. Think about that...Wow! The Creator of the Universe believes in you. Now...I hope you're saying, "This is *MY* Monday and I will treat it as I treat myself; Good." (Hey Friend, I'm making MY Monday a good one, glad you are too ☺!) Yay!

Today is Trade Tuesday!

Today is TRADE TUESDAY! Did you know that you can Trade with yourself? Yes, you surely can. I've spent much of a lifetime doing that, and still do. I've been known to carry some heavy baggage around in my earlier years. Finally, I decided to Trade them for a light heart, which I'd heard could happen with Trader Jesus Christ. Sure enough, He took my bags of clutter and presented me with the miracle of peace! So, through life, I make it a habit to be a Trader. Every day to me is a Trade day. I trade disappointment for satisfaction. Dismay for relief. Aggravation for calm. Do you see what I mean? How do I make that happen? Only one sure way; three little words I've come to love and count on. IN HIS STRENGTH. Works for me. It'll work for you, too. Be a Trader! You'll love it!

Today is Warranty Wednesday!

Today is WARRANTY WEDNESDAY! We all know what a Warranty is, but let's spell it out. When you buy an appliance or vehicle, etc., for instance, you get a warranty that guarantees it to last a certain amount of time, and if it doesn't, certain parts will be replaced at no cost. Analogy here: When you receive Salvation through Jesus your Savior, the Warranty guarantees you a Home in Heaven that lasts forEVER and EVER, and you won't need ANYthing replaced! All your "parts" will be perfected. What a deal! What a Warranty! Get your Salvation today! It's already purchased! You can pick it up at the foot of the Cross of Calvary. Jesus Christ will meet you there! As a matter of a fact, the blood He shed paying for your salvation is already there waiting for you!

Today is Think Thursday!

Today is THINK THURSDAY! You are breathing, right? You know that the very next breath could be your last, right? When that happens, you will live FOR ETERNITY in either one of two places. Think about eternity. Think about Forever in an awesome place or Forever in utter torment. Duh...Are you *really* thinking now?

Today is Favor Friday!

Today is FAVOR FRIDAY! (A token of love; to treat with kindness; to show partiality towards; regards shown by a superior/approving consideration). I think you get it. We all like having Favor from certain people in our lives, don't we? It's natural. I'd like to tell you a short story about Favor...One night my husband and I were traveling from Memphis to Nashville, Tennessee, and I was dozing. (He said that's what I did best on a trip ☺.) He later told the story, "I started praying, asking God to meet this need, that need, do this, please do that, and all of a sudden I realized all I had done was give God a wish-list. With that, I just said, 'Lord, forget all I've been saying...All I really want...is to find Favor with you.'" (The next day, Ray wrote the song, "Let Me Find Favor".) Friends, that says it all. Our Heavenly Father is the most important One – ever – to give us Favor. Do you have His Favor on this Friday?

Today is Sweep Saturday!

Today is SWEEP SATURDAY! Okay, time to get that broom out and start sweeping through your life and home a little. (Something that should be done periodically, actually.) You'll know which areas need to be swept clear of stuff more than others. Yes, you *do* know. So, grab that broom and get busy, Buster (or Busterette ☺.) Sweep!

Today is State Sunday!

Today is STATE SUNDAY! What State do YOU live in? I'll tell you what state I live in; a new state of mind! I've mentioned before that I was saved at age seven, but as an adult, I've made sure that I knew I was. Re-committed my life to Jesus, etc. I received a new state of mind as an adult, and it was an amazing feeling! You know, we step into different states of mind when troubles and sorrows come, when happiness and gladness is with us, etc. But the good thing is that we can ALWAYS be in a Spiritual State of Mind, and the Bible is the map we use to help us handle all of the other states as we travel through them! Let me ask you again, what State are you in right now...?

Week 49

Today is Momentum Monday!

Today is MOMENTUM MONDAY! (The strength or force that allows something to continue or to grow stronger or faster as time passes.) Any of you Readers who walk for exercise know that you always feel better after the first tenth of a mile. You get your Momentum going. But there's one thing that has a momentum which I dislike, and that's gossip. No, this Blurb is not about gossip, but it IS about Momentum, and when there's gossip, momentum is just gonna be involved, because the devil is gonna see to that. Gossip is when you know something about somebody that you don't need to be telling, or especially something you just "heard" from someone else and now you're passing it on. What happens is that same story has gained momentum and the proportions get out of shape and are destined pretty much to hurt whoever this story is about. Momentum can be good...if it's something that's positive. Momentum is bad if it's negative. And, my Reader Friend, you have a conscience and you *know* when you need to STOP the Momentum of the bad. (You *do* know, too!)

Today is Timely Tuesday!

Today is TIMELY TUESDAY! (Done or occurring at a favorable or useful time; opportune.) In days gone by, friends or loved ones could come to visit you and not feel it necessary to let you know they were coming beforehand. It's different in today's world for most folks, though. Everyone is so busy with their own agendas and lives that are filled to the brim with this and that, there's not much time for visiting anymore. We almost have to have an invitation to gather for some much-needed fellowship. Well, changes come and we just have to make the best of it. At least we do have "contraptions," as my grandmother would say, that allow us to contact our relatives and friends and let them know we need to meet! Cell phones! What would we do without them! I guess we can all praise the Lord for allowing us to live in an age of technology, because in a Timely manner, I – for one – can text my daughter and say, "I'm coming over, and I'll be there in thirty minutes! Tell my sweet son-in-law to go ahead and get the grill started ☺! Now, that's Timely, I would say. (At least for *me*, not sure about the Griller ☺!)

Today is Work Wednesday!

Today is WORK WEDNESDAY! No, not talking about laboring 9-5, but about working to make Life better. Easier. Fun. And it can be all of that! It takes putting forth effort, but it's worth it! Do you speak positive or negative statements? Do you quote scriptures to yourself during the day to help make different situations work? If you don't, you're not living the Good Life! All of the above will make your life easier as well as fun. The Bible guarantees it! Here's a favorite scripture that I just absolutely love: Mark 9:23 says, "*If thou canst believe, all things are possible to him that believeth.*" (I just love the word "canst," it's so "cool.") Look it up for yourself; it'll speak to you...! (Even better, it'll *Work* for you!)

Today is Tune Thursday!

Today is TUNE THURSDAY! Tuning in to the wonders of this earth is one of the greater privileges we have as humans. Being a singer/songwriter, it seems a tune stays in my mind a good part of the time. Sometimes one tune just "plays" over and over until I force myself to think of another one to take its place. Many folks "tune in" to a radio station so they can listen to some good music, or even a Talk Show. Can I share something with you? How do you think I wrote 365+ pages in this book!?! I "tuned in" to the One Above whom I knew could put words into my mind that He thought different people might need to hear. Lots of folks are tuned to birds chirping, while others tune in to the beauty of lilies in the fields and flowers in the garden. My husband always loved watching storms, but he tuned in to cloud formations even more. Today, Tune Thursday...There are all kinds of things you can Tune in to. You might even be a Tune for someone else, huh? (Hey, can you sing Jingle Bells for us ☺?)

Today is Field Friday!

Today is FIELD FRIDAY! Don't get upset, now. You're thinking that you're a City Guy and what is this Field Friday gonna be about! We're not going to talk about pastures and fields in the country today, so you can just relax, okay 🙂? Today's Blurb is to explain about a spiritual matter. Just hang on and receive, please. To set the stage, the world is thought of – to Christians – as a "field" that needs to be harvested. Sinners need to be brought into the Kingdom, just as hay needs to be harvested from the field to the barn. The deal is, when you become a Christian, a corner of that field becomes YOURS, my Friend, to harvest. Yes! Your own corner. How do you harvest a sinner? Tell them how Jesus saves; He shed His blood and died on the cross for every sinner, so that we could go to Heaven and live there for eternity. Lead them in the sinner's prayer: "Lord Jesus, I believe that you are the Son of God. Forgive me for my sins and come into my heart. I will serve you the rest of my life." When you have "harvested" this sinner, share your heart with another one. God will bless you for what you're doing for Him in your corner of the Field!

Today is Schedule Saturday!

Today is SCHEDULE SATURDAY! In today's world we seem to be schedule-minded 24/7. We get in a work-sleep-work cycle. We need to block time off for fun somewhere! Go to dinner with a friend/friends, take a class that's offered for free on "How To," just get in your car or pickup and ride through the country, go to a museum, well, you get the idea. Schedule time for fun! It's like having a mini-vacation. It refreshes. Fun has been one of the best meds I've ever been prescribed! Now, I'm prescribing it to you! Schedule some fun!

Today is Sacred Sunday!

Today is SACRED SUNDAY! (Highly valued and important; entitled to everence.) I figure I can name some things that are Sacred to most people. Parents, siblings, spouses, children, grands, greats, your church, and your church family. As humans we naturally think of our loved ones first. Now, let's get to some more aspects of the word sacred. The main item that's even beyond sacred is your Bible. God's Word. Where He speaks to you. How cool is that! Speaking from every verse! For sure don't forget, your own life is very sacred to God who created you. Lots of things in this world are sacred to different people. Sports are sacred to some folks. Gambling is to others, for instance. Not all sacred choices are best for folks. What's Sacred to you?

Week 50

Today is Monitor Monday!

Today is MONITOR MONDAY! Those who have computers are familiar with Monitors. Same with nurses and doctors; complex/wonderful machines monitor oxygen, heart rate, blood pressure, etc. For years schools have people who "monitor" the halls, offsetting any trouble they might see. Security cameras monitor doors and hallways as well as outside areas for different buildings. But...the monitors that fascinate me more than any...are the mind and heart. "What!?!" you say. "Absolutely," I reply. Just think about it. Your heart starts to fall in love with someone and your mind recognizes what's happening and says to your heart, "Be careful now, go slow; you don't want to get hurt." Same with shopping for a new puppy. Your heart says, "Oh, he's so adorable!" Your mind says, "Yes, he is, but he's too big for your toddler." Your mind is an incredible monitor and your heart is precious! A great example of your Heart Monitor; if your *mind* is checking to see if Jesus is living in your heart, you can be assured your *heart* will say, "You don't have to check anymore; I *know* He's here because I *feel* Him!" Aren't our Monitors just *incredible*!?!

Today is Thumbs Tuesday!

Today is THUMBS TUESDAY! I guess we've all had days when we feel like we're "all thumbs." Ladies drop an egg they are about to scramble, drop our needle trying to sew on a button, can't put on makeup as smoothly and quickly, and men drop screws, hammer thumbs instead of the nail, and the list keeps growing. Basically, our fingers don't seem to be able to cooperate with our brain and we just get clumsy for seemingly no reason, ever so often. Truth is, "all thumbs" is not always physical. This "plight" might hit us when we're about to do a Presentation at work, when we need to talk to a friend about a sensitive subject, etc., plus I'm sure all of you Readers have your own incidents you can remember where your mind just wasn't as smooth as usual. You felt like you were "all thumbs." Well, here's what I've learned: If you pray (Truly!) before you attempt ANY job, be it cooking breakfast, building a shelf or anything else, chances are great your efforts will go smoother. For so long I thought it was foolish to pray before every little chore/job. Until I learned better. Go ahead, put your mental Thumbs to work...with some sincere prayers. Works for me; it'll work for you. Your Thumbs will act nice for you ☺.

Today is Witty Wednesday!

Today is WITTY WEDNESDAY! You can make a witty, positive or funny statement to someone that will brighten their day. Most of us try to make others laugh anyway. So, let's make an effort to do just that today, tomorrow, and the rest of the week! Too many "down" situations in the world facing us – so we need funny, Witty "ups" from anybody and everybody! YOU are Anybody and YOU are Everybody...LOL! You are Witty today ☺!

Today is Temple Thursday!

Today is TEMPLE THURSDAY! I'm always surprised to hear about someone who doesn't have a clue that their body is a Temple. Scripture, 1 Corinthians 6:19-20 spells it out: *"What? know ye not that your body is the temple of the Holy Ghost (which is) in you, which ye have of God, and ye are not your own? For ye are bought with a price. Therefore, glorify God in your body, and in your spirit, which are God's."* Wow! God created our bodies and they belong to Him. How do you glorify Him with *your* body/Temple? Do you take care of it? Hey, have you *asked* Him to help you do that?

Today is Favorite Friday!

Today is FAVORITE FRIDAY! Do you have a favorite breed of dog? Favorite flavor of ice cream? Favorite color? Vehicle? (Men will have a long list of favorite trucks☺!) Have a favorite movie or book? We could list favorites all day long but you know what? It's Friday and time to make plans for the weekend. If you're sitting quietly thinking about all the things you MUST do, and NEED to do, just ignore them and for once think about some of your *favorite* things to do. Just make sure, though, that going to church and keeping the Sabbath Holy is on the list, and make it *always* one of your FAVORITE things to do! God will bless you for remembering Him and His commandments!

Today is Sustenance Saturday!

Today is SUSTENANCE SATURDAY! (Nourishment.) I've already alluded to this before, that food and water is a must for us to live. Without it, we'll just fade away and die. But there are also other requirements for a healthy life for some folks. They need "people-nourishment," and it's to feed their emotional requirements. So, they might bowl with others, ride in a horseback club, go fishing with a buddy, have a quilting or knitting group, etc. That's all great, especially if it provides a necessary Sustenance for your spirit. Yes, let's all feed ourselves with good nutrients! *And for sure*, let's be certain to feed ourselves daily with the best Sustenance of all! The answer to our needs, yours and mine: The Word of God. We have to have it to find our way through life. It feeds us, and without communing with God, we fade away and die spiritually. Did you know the Bible tells you that you cannot live by bread alone? Surely does. In Mathew 4:4. Read it and see if you don't believe me! Neighbor, feed yourself well today...on Sustenance Saturday and for every day for the rest of your life!

Today is Sturdy Sunday!

Today is STURDY SUNDAY! (Firm, resolute, stable.) I hope today will be a sturdy one for you in every way. One way to help that happen is to begin it with prayer. Have I ever told y'all how I learned to pray? To "*really*" pray? There's no long story behind my lesson. Simply, one day I realized God knew Laura and all her inner "makings" much better than Laura did. So, my next prayer began in that vein, coming from that knowledge. "Father, I trust *you* with this situation. *You* know my innermost feelings better than I do, so guide me, please." My Friends, when you get to the point when you can recognize that God knows what you need and what you don't, that He knows how you *really* feel in your spirit and soul, THEN you can pray more clearly and honestly! You have that "Sturdy" and stable feeling...when you pray like that. Think about what I've said...and try it.

Week 51

Today is Mountain Monday!

Today is MOUNTAIN MONDAY! There's *such* grandeur in mountains, and I love them. Sometimes the trials in our lives seem like mountains, but when you compare them with what Jesus did for us, I think you'll find that our mountains are really just hills. I hope this song I wrote will show you what I mean. "*Sometimes I see through eyes of sorrow, A problem that reaches the sky, And, it seems every day it gets bigger and bigger, A mountain that's too hard to climb. It's then I'm reminded of the story of Jesus, How He stood such a painful ordeal, So, my troubles all crumble and I know I can make it, 'Cause my mountain is only a hill.*" I hope these words will lodge in your heart and be there when you need them. This might feel like a Mountain Monday, but it's really a *HILL* Monday!

Today is Threshold Tuesday!

Today is THRESHOLD TUESDAY! (A level or point marking the start of something, the beginning point.) Life doesn't always go the way we've planned; I've already said that more than once in this book in different places. But let me reinforce it one more time. We can meet the challenges of change with gusto and the confidence of "I can do this," or we can whine, or let it depress us. After all, we're human. Imperfect. But just think of change like this: You're standing on the Threshold of a brand new "Life-Adventure!" If it has to happen, then for goodness sakes, embrace it with the best attitude you can give it! Remember when you got married and stepped across the Threshold? You experienced a feeling of a "Beginning to Something Wonderful." Because *YOU* vowed to make it wonderful. So...this change? Or the next change that comes your way? (And there will be one at some point, of some kind.) Bring up that same Wonderful Feeling! Stand on that Threshold and jump *into* the new change! You can do it!!! I would say Good Luck, but I'd rather say, "Be Blessed!"

Today is Worship Wednesday!

Today is WORSHIP WEDNESDAY! Why not put a Blurb about Worship on Sunday you may think. Well, because Worship starts with the letter W instead of S, that's why ☺. And besides that, my friend, what's wrong with worshipping God on Wednesday as well as Sunday! Nothing wrong, I'll tell you, and EVERYthing right! One way to worship God is to praise Him in both song, words from your lips, and from your prayers! Words from your heart. Psalms 22:3 says, "*God inhabits the praises of His people.*" That means when you praise Him, since God's presence is in our midst, He lives in your praises, your prayers! That's just awesome! Right this minute, if you start praising Him, for instance just say, "I love you, Lord, and I know that you are an awesome God," He is alive right then, in your heart, mind, and all around you! So, my Friends, get your church duds on and *get excited* about walking into your church to do some praising and Worshiping! God will bless you for it!

Today is Tackle Thursday!

Today is TACKLE THURSDAY! (To seize, take hold of with intention of subduing or stopping). Don't even hesitate; *Tackle* those thoughts. *You* know the ones you were having about eating that second donut, about telling that co-worker a thing or two, about smoking that cigarette. (You gave them up three months ago, don't give in now!) Don't give in to negativism, to bad temptation. You can go one more day just by Tackling the thought! Picture you on the ball field, tackling the other side. That'll help you succeed in doing this. See? You did it! Hey, did you notice who that was helping you Tackle? It was the Holy Spirit...of *course*!

Today is Foundation Friday!

Today is FOUNDATION FRIDAY! (A basis upon which something stands.) Several "pictures" come to my mind's eye when I use the word Foundation; probably yours, too. The foundation of a house being built. The "faithful few" which make up the backbone of a church congregation. Newlyweds ready to build a family. Most important of all, God's Word. If you're going to have a successful life, you need the best foundation. Reminds me – maybe you, too ☺ – of the story we heard as children, about the Three Little Pigs. The wolf came and blew down the houses of two of them, because they didn't build their homes on strong enough foundations. The third little pig did. Wolf couldn't blow it down. Great foundation. You want a Godly home that won't allow Satan to blow it apart? It's simple. Make sure you and your spouse are God's Children, live according to the Word, raise your family according to it, and make Life decisions from it. Voila! There it is. "*The*" Foundation to choose!

Today is Surety Saturday!

Today is SURETY SATURDAY! (Certainty.) What Surety do you have? In your faith? In your spouse? In your pastor? In your country? My husband, Ray, was as patriotic as the most dedicated soldier that's ever lived. He took what's happened to our nation in the past years with almost a personal pain. My opinion is that feeling goes with the territory of being patriotic. At least for one who's been a soldier, guarding our country. But Ray's faith in God was admirable and he knew that God is aware of every little thing going on in the world and will always be in control. I feel the same way. Of a Surety. Although my faith in some of our leaders has been shaken, my faith in God will never be moved. Ever. What about yours? I want you to think about how strong/sure your faith is because our country is facing some tough times and they're not likely to change much for the better. Is your faith – of a Surety – strong enough in God? Hang on to Him! He's the ONLY One – of a Surety – that can see us through until we're in Heaven!

Today is Synergy Sunday!

Today is SYNERGY SUNDAY! (Combined action or operation; working together.) Awesome to belong to an international group called Christians. Notice the word action. Means busy. Doing. Helping the sick or needy, the orphans and the widows. Spreading the Gospel of Christ. Sooooo many ways to do that in the world of technology we have at our fingertips in this age of Time. Working together serving Him is the greatest job you could ever have! Believe it! Create your synergy today!

Week 52

Today is Mindful Monday!

Today is MINDFUL MONDAY! I'm going to tell you about how "Mindful" I found God to be. I found a mint green straight skirt made from that swingy material I just love, and I knew a black top and black heels would make it look nice. One day a month or two later I was shopping, and I couldn't believe what I was seeing! A pair of black heels with mint green polka dots all over them! I just loved them! Had to have them. NOW I had an awesome outfit. Another few weeks passed and again, were my eyes deceiving me? There – right in front of me – was a scarf. Not just ANY scarf. A black scarf with mint green polka dots on it!!! Couldn't believe it! I grabbed it! Could this be any more thrilling for me? No ☺, not for *this* lady. I now had the ultimate outfit. Then it hit me. WHAT, I ask you, were the chances of my finding those heels and scarf to compliment my skirt and top? None. Unless...it was the Holy Spirit. And of course, I realized, it was! God is *so* mindful. He knows I love things like that, so...He delighted in blessing me. Because He loves me. And *wow*, do I love *Him*!!!!! A Mindful God! What about that! (Below is the actual outfit, though the mint colors and dots don't come through too well.)

Today is Twister Tuesday!

Today is TWISTER TUESDAY! No need for a definition on that word for sure. First thing that comes to our minds, most likely, is a tornado, since they're called "twisters" much of the time. They'll twist anything in their path, and cause terrible damage, with heartache to follow. Parallel: Your enemy, the devil, is a Master Twister. John 10:10 says, "*The thief comes to steal and kill and destroy*." So, make no mistake about it, folks, the devil is truly a twister. He will ruin your life and the lives of your loved ones if you allow it! Good thing about this is that God has control over this twister, so turn your life over to Him, love Him, trust Him and, no matter what happens, He will keep you in His Hand until you are in His presence...in Heaven. Good news! No Twisters in Heaven!

Today is Wear Wednesday!

Today is WEAR WEDNESDAY! It's close to the end of the year. I wish that I could see everyone right now that's reading this Blurb. So I could see your countenance. I wish I knew if any of these Blurbs have helped you in any way. Maybe you Wear a smile more than you used to. Or even a grin. Or you're chuckling. Laughing a lot more? I wish every one of you all the happiness you can help to bring to your life. We'll never all meet each other here on this earth, but from the bottom of my heart I hope that I will see you in Heaven. You might come up to me and say, "I read your book, Laura Livingston Lewis," and I'll just hug you and say, "I'm sooooo tickled to meet you!" Guess what...We'll *ALL* be wearing a smile then!!! Awesome! All you Readers? You have touched my heart just by getting my book. Touched my heart, truly. I never planned to write one, but God planned it for me. He's amazing. God bless each one of you! I mean that...

Today is Tint Thursday!

Today is TINT THURSDAY! (To color something slightly; tinge.) Are some of your days less than "full color?" Your spirit is tinted with cloudy instead of sunshine? First thing I'd ask you is, "Why?" Is it that you do not have friends and family? I understand if that's your life. However, one way to think of that is this: You're not the only one. There are millions of folks on this same earth as you who have no family, either. As for friends, there are also millions of people in the world who would be willing to be your friend. And even if it isn't easy to reach out and make a friend, if you want your life to be fuller, richer, then you might have to make the first move. Now: Let's say you just don't want to do that, but you still need your life tinted with a little more color. Okay. There's the Internet with all kinds of music to listen to that will bring a tap to your foot. A spring to your step. Videos to watch that will do the same thing if you choose the right ones. That's the important word, you see. Choose. Choice. Life is about choices. To Tint your life with more color or not to Tint it. If you're smart enough to be reading this book, then you're intelligent enough to choose good things for yourself! I have faith in you! *You can do it*. Go ahead. Make the first choice of how to Tint. Have fun choosing!!!

Today is Follow Friday!

Today is FOLLOW FRIDAY! We Follow this and that, not giving "stuff" much thought. One thing I've learned about following is that a lot of people lean towards a particular political party because their parents did. Because their parents did? No, we're not going to argue politics here, but I do want to point out something about you, *IF* you're guilty of the above. You are not the same person as your parents. Politics – as we once knew it – has been slowly changing through the years, and not in a good direction! Poor George Washington and all of those that went through hard times to found this country would rise from their graves if they knew what has happened to their United States! Though you know politics have changed, you feel obligated to "stick to what Mama and Daddy believed." Mercy! Surely you have a mind of your own. Don't you want to look at the facts and make a conscious choice of your own? Wake up! You're part of America! *It needs you* to follow the leaders who were directed by God in forming this country, and that certainly included leaning on the Bible's instructions. Do you vote according to your faith in those instructions? Just wondering...just wondering...

Today is Strong Saturday!

Today is STRONG SATURDAY! The word Strong doesn't necessarily mean in physical strength, and most of us know that. My former pastor said something once that was *so* great. He said he was talking with his son about Life one day and he told his son, "Men are not made in the Fitness Center; they're made in the closet." Oh, how true that is. When a person goes into their personal "prayer closet" and it's just them and the Lord, that Heavenly Father will show you some things. He'll build your mind and heart to be strong. In the quiet, you can hear His still small voice...guiding you. Growing you. Helping you to be a man or a woman He can be proud of. Guess what: Today that same "son" is now my pastor (same church) and his father was right. Men are made in the closet. My current pastor must've stayed in that closet a lot because he's a chip off the old block. (His father, who was and still is a great minster of the Gospel, now traveling and teaching around the world.) So, Fathers and Mothers? Make room in your teens' closets for a place to kneel...

Today is Seek Sunday!

Today is SEEK SUNDAY! If you don't get anything else from this book, I hope you'll let this particular Blurb speak to you. Just letting you know, God is a gentleman. He won't force Himself on you. He already gives you air to breathe, a mind with free will, etc. With that free will, He's actually sitting on his Throne in Heaven, watching you, waiting for you to seek Him. Ask about Him. Learn about Him and His Word, the Bible. Here's a few scriptures that will help you see what I'm talking about: Jeremiah 29:13 says, "*And ye shall seek me, and find me, when ye shall search for me with all your heart.*" Psalm 119: 2 is another you'll want to read. Deuteronomy 4:29 is good, and Proverbs 8:17 is great!!! Matthew 7:7-8, 1 Chronicles 16:11, and Lamentations 3:25 are more. *Wonderful* verses from the God who created this vast, incredible Universe! Read these and talk to Him. Don't put it off. He's waiting...

Holidays

Today
is
New Year's Day...
(Welcome Day!)

Today is WELCOME DAY! "Welcome to the New Year I have given you! I love you and I had a great time creating you! I only want the best for you, so keep me in your heart and we'll walk this journey through Life together," is what your Heavenly Father is saying right now! Folks, there are kings in many countries on this earth. It would take you a "month of Sundays" to speak with them, if ever. But...the King of Kings, the King of ALL of the earthly kings, is available ANYtime 24/7 to speak with you! And *WANTS* to speak with you! This year is brand new, my friends. Isn't it awesome? A new year full of new opportunities, new blessings, new choices. Though the year date has changed, God has not! He's the same this year as He was last year, and since the beginning of Time. What a comfort to know He loves us year in and year out. Now: This year's commitment? Love *HIM* more!!! You can. Talk to Him! Will you...?

Today is Valentine's Day…
(Sappy Day!)

Today is SAPPY DAY! (Foolishly sentimental.) Well, how about it, are you ready to grin a little today? Sappy can be a good thing. Let's say you're not one to say, "I love you" to your spouse a lot. Guess I'd mostly be talking to the men on this one, wouldn't I. That's because you're "macho," of course. Most men don't get "sappy" with their feelings. But why not, I demand! Why not look at your wife or girlfriend with love in your eyes and let her know just how much she means to you! Sappy can bring you a lot of rewards if you'll just think about it ☺. So, be it male or female, let this day be one that will make memories for you because you decided to get "out of the box" and be Sappy. You're entitled to do that, you see, because this is Sappy Valentine's Day! (Get those lips puckered ☺.)

Today is Easter Sunday…
(Symbolize Sunday!)

Today is SYMBOLIZE SUNDAY! (Represent or express.) To Christians, Easter Sunday is the day symbolized in honor of when Jesus Christ arose from the tomb, after He was crucified three days before that. Just think about it...He's alive today! We're so happy to celebrate that day, although it's not on the same Sunday every year. Jesus lives in Heaven, where He ascended over two thousand years ago, to prepare a place for His family. Us. We can only imagine the thrill that Mary felt when she learned that Jesus was not in the tomb, then the Disciples joy when He appeared unto them! Mercy me! I would've shouted (or probably fainted would be more like it☺) if I'd been there! We Christians are sooooooo blessed to serve a Lord that's alive, and who loves us. His Spirit lives within us and all around us. Right now! Just look around you! Feel Him? He's here! Time to celebrate what we Symbolize...Easter! Christ is arisen! Can I shout now? Whoooohoooo and yeeeehaw!!! (That's the way I shout☺.)

Today is Mother's Day…
(Sacrifice Sunday!)

Today is SACRIFICE SUNDAY! The first thing I think of when I hear the word Sacrifice is Jesus, of course. That's a given. But I also think of my mother, and that's understandable because of Mother's Day. I have memories of things she did while I was growing up which I had no idea at the time were sacrifices for her family. I'm glad they were imprinted in my mind because after I grew up and got out into life, they let me know just how much she loved us and what a woman of worth she was, to make the sacrifices she did. One picture that stands out in my mind is in the kitchen at the big table where my dad and siblings were seated. She stood over by the stove so much of the time with her plate, nibbling. Years later as I brought up the memories, I realized she was just making sure we all had enough to eat before she'd sit down. I'm sure now that many times she gave up some of her portion for us. You see, there were ten of us children. So, sacrifice? Yes. She's in Heaven now, but to me she's Mother of the Year. Know what we put on her headstone? "The Original Steel Magnolia." Happy Mother's Day to all Mother's everywhere! Even if you're a Mother of the heart, this wish is for you, too!

Today is Memorial Day...
(Memorial Monday!)

This is MEMORIAL MONDAY! (Serving to preserve remembrance; commemorative; a memento, keepsake). This whole Memorial Day holiday will not be celebrated because of Bar-B-Q, hot dogs, or off from work, but its greatness comes from why it's a holiday in the first place. A lot of blood was shed for you to be here in this nation standing out there, bar-b-queing with your friends and family during the next few days! I hope that before you take your first bite, you'll remember to thank God He gave us America in the first place, and for those men who've been willing for over two-hundred years to fight for our freedom and keep our nation safe! Then, you can start plowing into the food ☺!

Today is Father's Day...
(Father's Sunday!)

Today is FATHER'S SUNDAY! I'm very thankful for this special holiday each year. Our Heavenly Father created it for us, and when the day closes, I can always say that He's been with me the whole day in my blunders and mistakes, plus the good parts ☺. We couldn't ask for a better Father than our Father God. I can tell you a truth and it's that we should all celebrate Father's Day every day of the year, when it pertains to the Father Above. He's worthy. *More* than. Powerful and mighty. Rules the universe. Most of all...*LOVES US*! This year as you celebrate the Father's Day holiday, make sure you give great honor to the one who gave life to the earthly Father you'll be celebrating.

Today is Independence Day...
(Monumental Day!)

Today is MONUMENTAL DAY! On this day in 1776, the Thirteen Colonies declared their independence from England. This eventually led to the formation of the United States, and this is why we have reason to celebrate! On this day, I always give remembrance to the Pilgrims, who had a monumental day when they landed on these shores, made this unknown land their home and taught their children – and their children's children – to keep building it into a brand-new nation. If you're like me, then you thank the Lord for guiding the minds of the men who formed the Constitution for this "new" country. It was a Monumental day for them! Think how THEY must've celebrated!!! And today, America is still the land where freedom rings! (I had a Monumental July 4th one year when my youngest daughter was born, and I've told her, since she's been grown, that she was my "watermelon ☺." I tell her I was just being "Patriotic," having her on that holiday ☺.) Hope everyone has a great July 4th!

Today is Labor Day...
(Momentous Monday!)

Today is MOMENTOUS MONDAY! (Event of great importance.) The first Monday in Sepember, Americans observe this Momentous day to pay tribute to working men and women in the U.S. and Canada. Federal, state, and local governments close their offices, as do banks and post offices. It marks the end of summer, with backyard cookouts, etc. It's a great time for families and friends to gather and share love and appreciation for each other. *That's* momentous, nowadays! The first time I heard the word "labor" I was eight years old. My mother sent my brother and me to the nearest neighbor that had a phone. We carried a note (We read it ☺.) that said, "I am in labor. Please call my doctor," and gave his number. After reading the note, we wondered to each other what "labor" meant. Had no idea it was going to mean a new baby brother☺! Today, I can tell you after four children, I know what labor means ☺. So, on this Monday, relax! Except for those manning the grill, that is ☺. (All Mama's, don't forget to make your Banana Pudding!)

Today is Halloween…
(Treat, No Trick Day!)

Today is TREAT, NO TRICK DAY! And shame on you if you trick on Halloween, no matter what day of the week it falls on each year! Enough troubles today without someone deliberately playing a trick on you! Let's use Halloween season to treat Jesus, whaddaya think!!! Cool, huh? Start thinking now: How many ways can you treat (bless) Him...?

Today is Thanksgiving…
(Thankful Thursday!)

Today is THANKFUL THURSDAY! (Grateful, appreciative.) In many homes today, a tradition is kept. Families gather for a big meal and to have time to enjoy each other. That's great. Many families sit down at the table and before they ask the blessing over the feast, a chance is given for each member to tell what they're thankful for. That's such a great thing to do on that day, but let's talk...What are you really thankful for? Most will put their family first, then go from there, which is understandable. But don't you think you should put your Heavenly Father at the top of that list, *then* your family? If it weren't for Him, you wouldn't *have* a family! He's in control of everything in our lives, including making a way for everything you're thankful for...today. Now the prayer has been said and it's time for Grandpa to carve the turkey. Let's eat! Happy Thanksgiving, Everyone!

Today is Christmas Day…
(First-Class Day!)

Today is FIRST-CLASS DAY! We don't need a dictionary to tell us the meaning of that, do we! We know what first-class is. However, I'll elaborate on what First-Class means on this particular day. Christmas Day! (You're probably ahead of me in your thoughts, but I'll continue, anyway.) Christians celebrate Christmas as the day Christ Jesus was born. He might've been born in a stable with animals around, but He was still First-Class! That's why the angels rejoiced and the guiding star was in the sky. The King of Kings was born! He came to earth to save us all from our sins (Thanks to Adam and Eve) and make provisions for us to go to Heaven, at least those that believe He is the Son of God. Just want everybody to know that I'm FIRST-CLASS because I'm a Child of the King! I hope you're First-Class, too! Merry Christmas, Everybody!

Today is New Year's Eve...
(Tidal Day!)

Today is TIDAL DAY! I'm a little sad since this is the last writing for my book. I wonder if I have conveyed everything I'd hoped in the beginning, which was simply, "If I have made it through many crushing trials in Life, I know you can, too!" Then I hear that still, small voice of the Lord reminding me of *parts* of different verses in Ecclesiastes 3: "*To everything there is a season, and a time to every purpose under the heaven, a time to plant, a time to build up, a time to laugh, a time to embrace, and a time to speak,*" etc., and the scriptures continue. This was my season to write this book. Folks, I call this Tidal Day because that's what Life is. Ins and outs, with ups and downs, but giving it our best. Failing at times, succeeding at others. Never giving up! Meeting each day with fresh Grace from God, learning to be wise in using His strength – which He freely gives – to sail through the challenges Life gives us. The tides come and go, but we're good Sailors. That is, we are *if* we sail...in *His* strength. My Friends...Go with God!

Acknowledgements

My heartfelt thanks to my Editors:

JoAnn Quitmeyer: JoAnn, when I started this book in 2011, I had no idea you even existed. God knew, though, and He alone is responsible for putting us together! How blessed I am to call you my friend! (My Publisher/Editor).

Henrietta Brown, I couldn't have done this without your professional expertise! Your industry skills speak for themselves: More than 40 years in printing, publishing, graphic design, editing, writing. (Mother of two, mother-in-law of two, grandmother of one.) "Thankful every day, for Joy in the Journey!" (My Editor)

My Heavenly Father, who inspired this book and molded me to be an Encourager.

Laura

About the Author

Laura Livingston Lewis is a Gospel singer/songwriter (aka Laura Lewis). In addition to the hundreds of songs she has written, Laura has been a feature writer for both *The Gospel Voice Magazine* and *The US Gospel News*. Four of her songs became "career" songs for four different recording artists, bringing them to the forefront of the nation. She has been on four different major TV networks, reaching over 180 countries. Her husband Ray is in Heaven following a courageous battle with cancer. Laura tours the country ministering in songs, which she calls "little three-minute messages." You can find her videos on YouTube: Take Ten #1 by Laura Lewis" (For additional videos use #2, #3, etc.) In her spare time, Laura enjoys reading, photography, and writing. She lives in the Nashville, Tennessee area, and would love your emails: lauralivingstonlewis@gmail.com

www.ingramcontent.com/pod-product-compliance
Lightning Source LLC
Chambersburg PA
CBHW060044230426
43661CB00004B/654